YOU DON'T HAVE TO BE BAD TO

GET BETTER

YOU DON'T HAVE TO BE BAD TO

GET BETTER

A Leader's Guide to Improving Teacher Quality

CANDI B. McKAY

Foreword by Charlotte Danielson

CORWIN
A SAGE Company

CORWIN
A SAGE Company

FOR INFORMATION:

Corwin
A SAGE Company
2455 Teller Road
Thousand Oaks, California 91320
(800) 233-9936
www.corwin.com

SAGE Publications Ltd.
1 Oliver's Yard
55 City Road
London EC1Y 1SP
United Kingdom

SAGE Publications India Pvt. Ltd.
B 1/I 1 Mohan Cooperative Industrial Area
Mathura Road, New Delhi 110 044
India

SAGE Publications Asia-Pacific Pte. Ltd.
3 Church Street
#10-04 Samsung Hub
Singapore 049483

Acquisitions Editor: Debra Stollenwerk
Associate Editor: Desirée A. Bartlett
Editorial Assistant: Kimberly Greenberg
Production Editor: Laura Barrett
Copy Editor: Brenda White
Typesetter: C&M Digitals (P) Ltd.
Proofreader: Jennifer Gritt
Indexer: Jean Casalegno
Cover Designer: Gail Buschman
Permissions Editor: Adele Hutchinson

Copyright © 2013 by Corwin

Printed in the United States of America

Library of Congress Cataloging-in-Publication Data

McKay, Candi B.

You don't have to be bad to get better : a leader's guide to improving teacher quality / Candi B. McKay.

p. cm.
Includes bibliographical references and index.

ISBN 978-1-4522-4087-9 (pbk.)

1. Educational leadership. 2. School principals. 3. Educational accountability. I. Title.

LB2831.6.M35 2013
371.2—dc23   2012041625

This book is printed on acid-free paper

MIX
Paper from
responsible sources
FSC® C014174

13 14 15 16 17 10 9 8 7 6 5 4 3 2 1

Contents

Foreword   ix

Preface   xi

Acknowledgments   xv

About the Author   xvii

1. Removing the Rose-Colored Glasses   1

The Rose-Colored Glasses Phenomenon   1
   Red Flag Warnings   3
   Demonstrating Moral Courage   6
Leading Change: Necessary Dispositions   7
   Perceptions About the Role of a School Leader   7
   Confidence in Self as an Instructional Leader   10
   A Growth Mindset   11
   Moral Courage   13
Key Points About Removing the Rose-Colored Glasses   14
Putting Words Into Action   15
   Reflecting on Your Current State   15
   Action Tools   16

2. No More Lake Wobegon: Creating a Culture of Learning   19

The Effects of Well-Intended Fiction: A Culture of Nice   19
The Changing Landscape   21
The Leader's Role: Essential Beliefs and Understandings   22
   Changing Beliefs: Practice Comes First!   22
   Drinking the Water   24
   Understanding About Learning   26
   A Presumption of Continuous Growth for All   27

Setting the Stage: Defining Who We Are   28
    Capturing the School's History   28
    Developing Core Beliefs and Commitments   30
Demonstrating Beliefs: Actions of the School Leader   32
    Developing Trust and Rapport   32
    Step Aside and Lead: Creating Opportunities for Learning 34
Key Points About Creating a Culture of Learning   35
Putting Words Into Action   36
    Reflecting on Your Current State   36
    Action Tools   37

3. The Wisdom of Instructional Leadership:
What Leaders Need to Know and Do   **39**

Knowledge of Staff   40
Understandings About Teaching and Learning   43
    What Is Good Teaching?   43
    How Good Is Good Enough?   46
    How Does Learning Occur?   47
    What Is Engagement in Learning?   48
Skills of the Instructional Leader   51
    Collecting Evidence to Assess Teaching   52
    Engaging in Professional Conversations   54
    Skillful Questioning   55
    Productive Listening   56
    Providing Feedback   57
    Facilitating Professional Goal Setting   58
Key Points About What Leaders Need to Know   59
Putting Words Into Action   60
    Reflecting on Your Current State   60
    Action Tools   60

4. The Wisdom of Instructional Practice:
What Teachers Need to Know   **65**

Playing a Guessing Game   65
Guessing Games Replaced by Transparency   66
    Understandings About Teaching and Learning   66
    Putting Your Know-How Into Action:
    A Cycle of Continuous Improvement and Growth   68
Don't Forget to Feed the Teachers!   71
A Plan for Teacher Learning   73
Key Points About What Teachers Need to Know   75

Putting Words Into Action 75
    Reflecting on Your Current State 75
    Action Tool 76

5. Promoting Teacher Learning: It's All Talk! **83**

Powerful Conversations 83
Setting the Stage 85
    Acknowledging the Leader's Dual Role 85
    Making Intentions Clear 87
Factors That Impact Conversations 89
    Rapport and Relationship With the Teacher 90
    The Developmental Level of the Teacher 91
    The School Culture 91
    The Data Collected About Teaching and Learning 92
    The Teacher's Mindset 93
    The Skills of the Leader Facilitating the Conversation 94
Leading Conversations: When, What, and How 95
    When to Talk 95
    What to Talk About 96
    How to Talk 97
Key Points About Promoting Teacher Learning 101
Putting Words Into Action 102
    Reflect on Your Current State 102
    Action Tool 102

6. Principals Can't Lead Alone:
The Role of the District Office **105**

Improving Instruction: Does the Central Office Matter? 105
    A Case in Point 106
Increased Accountability for Leaders 106
Creating a Culture for Professional Learning: A Case Study 107
    A Powerful First Impression 107
    A History of Principal Autonomy 109
    Getting the Right Members on the Team 110
    Learning for All Adults in the System 112
    Aligning School and District Goals and Priorities 112
    Teacher Evaluation a Tool for Teacher Learning 113
    Professional Development as the Fuel for the System 115
    Expanding Professional Learning Across the District 116
    Finding Time for Professional Learning 118
    Securing the Future of Leaders and the Professional Staff 118

Key Points About the Role of the District Office   120
Putting Words Into Action   120
   Action Tool   120
   Reflect and Assess   122

References   **123**

Index   **127**

Foreword

I n this important book, Candi McKay offers specific, concrete guidance to school leaders who are committed to improving the quality of teaching in their schools. She follows the logic of the argument recently pointed out in the report "The Widget Effect" which demonstrated that, in many school districts, 99 percent of teachers are judged to be performing at a satisfactory level or above, with the vast majority judged to be at the top of the rating scale. This would be excellent news (all of our teachers are great!) if it weren't for the fact that in these same districts, many students are not learning well. And if we accept (and we must, due to the strength of the underlying research) that the quality of teaching is the single most important school factor contributing to student learning, then we won't have improvements in the latter without improvements to the former.

There are, of course, many reasons for schools to have, and to persist in, an unrealistic picture of the quality of teaching, which are convincingly described in this book, from a persistence of "rose-colored glasses," to a culture of "nice," to a lack of clear criteria for defining and recognizing good teaching, to a focus among school leaders on the managerial (rather than the instructional) aspects of their roles. But more valuable than this analysis of the problem are the specific tools and resources provided for school leaders to enhance their skills in the critical area of instructional leadership.

The author has many years' experience working with school leaders in helping them work with their teachers to strengthen instructional practice—this is not a message being sent from an ivory tower by an academic but advice well-grounded in both research and experience. And it is grounded as well in an optimistic view of teachers and the profession, one that posits both the enormous complexity of teaching and the commitment of teachers to improve their practice.

In fact, all this is summed up in the title: "You don't have to be bad to get better." The premise of the book is that in an endeavor so inherently complex and demanding as teaching, it's never perfect; that no matter how good a lesson is, it could *always* be a bit better. And furthermore, it's part of the responsibility of every teacher, as it is for every professional, to be engaged in a career-long quest to do a better job tomorrow than was possible today. It's a view of teachers as *learners*, reflecting the same orientation of learning as active intellectual engagement that underpins the assumptions of the *Framework for Teaching* about student learning.

I welcome this book as a significant contribution to the essential work of practicing school leaders, offering them guidance, specific tools, and resources to strengthen their work in the one essential part of their roles, that of improving the quality of teaching, and therefore of learning, in their schools. Only if this happens will schools fulfill their critical mission of educating children to their highest potential.

Charlotte Danielson

Preface

Improving teacher quality—what does it take, and whose job is it anyway? A seemingly simple question reveals an exceedingly complex answer. Teaching is complex work. There is no silver bullet or recipe to becoming an accomplished teacher. It requires a career-long commitment to professional learning and growth. Any successful teacher will attest to this. To suggest that the quality of teaching could be improved is not to say teaching is of poor quality, but a reflection of the complexity of the work. In other words, *you don't have to be bad to get better!*

Whose responsibility is it for ensuring that teaching is of high quality? Can teaching improve in the absence of effective leadership? We know that of all the factors that impact student learning, the single most important one (that happens *in* the school) is the quality of the teacher. Long standing research has established this fact. We also know that school leadership directly impacts teacher effectiveness. But how much does leadership really matter? Researchers from the Universities of Minnesota and Toronto found that *leadership is second only to classroom instruction among all school-related factors that contribute to what students learn at school* (Leithwood, Louis, Anderson, & Walhstrom, 2004). The relationship between teacher quality, school leadership, and student learning is clear. Is there any question then, that to improve teacher quality, we must address the needs of school leaders?

A Laser-Like Focus

The central purpose of this book is to describe the attributes of school leaders that enable them to improve the quality of teaching and learning.

Currently, there is unprecedented attention and focus on teacher quality and how it is defined, measured, and reported. This book is about school leadership but with a laser-like focus on what it takes to develop, support, and sustain quality teaching in any school environment.

Effective leaders demonstrate certain qualities that enable them to overcome the challenges and obstacles they face each day and to create and sustain a learning environment, driven first and foremost by the needs of the students. They are compelled by a moral compass, a vision of professional learning, and they lead with a growth mindset, seeking new opportunities to learn and meet the challenges in this era of increasing accountability and change.

The federal funding initiative known as Race to the Top spurred comprehensive reforms in schools across the country. In an effort to increase the number of students who are college and career ready, state and local districts have adopted the Common Core State Standards to help ensure students' success in literacy, mathematics, and multiple areas of study. State and local districts are using student data to drive instruction and are implementing new, standards-based teacher and principal performance evaluation systems. These changes have the potential to transform teaching and learning, but *only in the presence of strong instructional leadership.*

What are the attributes of strong instructional leaders? How are they able to effect changes in teaching practice that has remained virtually the same for decades? This book presents a road map for school leaders focused on the essential elements of instructional leadership necessary to improve the quality of teaching and to sustain these improvements over time in a climate of increased accountability for both principals and teachers across the country.

Organization and Structure

Chapter One begins by addressing the need for school leaders to remove their rose-colored glasses and develop the moral courage needed to confront the status quo. This chapter provides specific examples of how school leaders at every level have demonstrated this quality and have successfully implemented significant changes in teaching and professional learning as well as those who have not. It will also address, in detail, the habits of mind or predispositions of school leaders who are able to create and sustain improvements in teaching.

Chapter Two describes how successful leaders apply these habits of mind to implement change in their schools and create a culture for learning. Based on a premise of continuous learning for all, Chapter Two provides detailed action steps school leaders can take to create a culture for learning and change existing mindsets that may fear constructive criticism and feedback. As a result, leaders will be able to engage teachers in the change process needed to improve the quality of teaching.

Chapter Three lays out, in detail, the essential understandings about learning that are central to instructional leadership. It begins with having knowledge of the staff. Much like a teacher needs to know their students, school leaders must know their teachers as learners and as people. The chapter also details the skills of instructional leadership, such as observing and collecting evidence of teaching, communicating with teachers, and providing them with resources for learning and growth. It includes a detailed discussion of a critical concept for school leaders, student engagement, distinguishing it from mere compliance in the classroom.

Chapter Four focuses on what teachers need to know so that they can be active participants in their own learning. Although it would be impossible to put everything teachers need to know into one chapter, it is essential that teachers have the same information as their school leaders regarding learning and what constitutes effective practice. This promotes transparency, essential for engaging teachers as active participants in their own professional growth. It describes what teachers need to know so that they are able to engage in self-assessment, reflection, and professional conversations with their leaders. The chapter provides a model of how to embed this learning within the school so that it is sustainable over time.

Chapter Five underscores the value of professional conversation in promoting teacher learning. It is not enough for leaders to know what to talk about with teachers. They need how to strategies for talking with teachers in ways that will promote professional learning. This essential chapter provides a protocol for conducting conversations with teachers as a follow up to formal and informal classroom visits. Most of the current literature dealing with classroom walkthroughs or mini-observations fails to stress the importance of collaborative professional conversations in the process. Successful use of the protocol is based on school leaders and teachers having the prerequisite understandings outlined in the previous chapters.

Chapter Six rounds out the book by examining the critical role the district office plays in improving teacher quality. The support and commitment of the central office to teacher effectiveness is essential for building leaders to have in their work with teachers. The chapter presents a case study of instructional leadership where the superintendent and central office leadership team have taken deliberate steps to support ongoing, job embedded learning for teachers as well as leaders from every level across the district.

Practical and Useful Features

Critical concepts are presented in a simple and easy to read style. Rather than presenting key ideas as theory, the use of practical examples give the reader just what they need for deeper understanding. Strategies and "how to" tips for implementing the ideas presented are woven throughout the book. Tools and forms such as an Instructional Leadership Inventory, Capturing the School's History, Teacher Evaluation Survey, and an Instructional Practice Self-Assessment allow the reader to put the critical concepts presented to immediate use. Activities the leader can immediately implement with teachers such as the Research Roundup, Understanding Student Engagement, and Developing Professional Goals are presented with specific examples, vignettes, and step-by-step directions.

"Key Points" at the end of each chapter reflects the important content presented with specific steps to engage teachers and leaders. Each chapter concludes with a section titled, "Putting Words Into Action." The intent is for leaders to begin to engage in their own professional development and growth by using the questions presented at the end of the chapter to reflect on the topics presented in the chapter and then try out some tools. Words are merely words without a plan of action. Before proceeding to the next chapter, consider "putting words into action."

Audience

Although the primary audience of this book is school leaders, it is a useful tool for any educator committed to promoting higher levels of learning for students and continuous learning for teachers. It is also an essential read for district level leaders who play a central role in supporting building principals. As schools across the country race to implement federal and state mandates for new and more rigorous principal and teaching effectiveness models, they are looking for a place to start. This book provides a valuable resource to school leaders as they seek to replace old thinking, habits, and mindsets where teachers are satisfied being satisfactory with a view that sees professional learning and growth as the primary responsibility of teachers.

Acknowledgments

This book was inspired by educators whom I have been privileged to know and work with throughout my career. Thank you for always putting students first, as demonstrated by your commitment, dedication, and continuous displays of moral courage and integrity. Thank you for believing in your students, for seeing them as individuals, and for demonstrating respect for their intellect and potential to learn. You have inspired my own professional growth and validated my belief in the power of a single teacher to impact the life of a student.

A big thanks goes to many colleagues who I have been fortunate to work with over the years. I have learned so much from my collaboration with you. Thanks for the great work you do in the service of improving teacher quality and student learning. I want to especially thank Valerie Henning-Piedmonte, a loyal friend and trusted colleague, who taught me through her deeds and conduct the meaning of moral courage. You are a tribute to what is good in education and a model for what every school leader should aspire to become. Thank you for your contributions to this book and to my own professional growth.

I owe a special thanks to Charlotte Danielson, a colleague, mentor, and friend who guided my initial work and whose own work in the field of education has made substantial contributions to improving teacher quality. Thank you for providing educators with the language and tools needed for continuous growth and professional learning. I have learned so much from you.

Thanks to all of the people at Corwin who encouraged me to write this book and believed in it enough to see it published. To Debbie Stollenwerk, my editor, thanks for the gentle pressure which coaxed me into putting my thoughts on paper and seeing this through. You knew I would write this book long before I actually believed it myself. I also want to acknowledge the reviewers of this book for your helpful insights and comments.

Finally, I want to acknowledge the people who have been most near and dear to me throughout this journey. I am blessed with the support and steadfast caring of friends and family members who have always had a ready ear and words of encouragement. Most important among these is my husband Tom. This book would not have been written without your love and support. You have always believed in me and encouraged me to follow my passion, regardless of the sacrifices we've had to make along the way. Thank you for your patience and never-ending support—I have always known that I am the lucky one. To my children Tommy and Kendall, you have been the real inspiration behind my work. Your experiences in school and in life guided my choice to become a teacher and to always respect the individual differences every student brings to learning. I am so proud of the honest, caring, successful adults you have become. Angela, your work ethic and drive to succeed in whatever you do inspires me. I am so thankful that you are part of our family. Cynthia, thank you for being in the world with me and for helping me see what has always been there. You are brilliant. Thanks for sharing some of that with me.

Publisher's Acknowledgments

Corwin would like to thank the following individuals for taking the time to provide their editorial insight and guidance:

Jo Blase, Corwin Author and Professor
The University of Georgia
Virginia Beach, VA

Frank Chiki, Principal
Chamiza Elementary School
Albuquerque, NM

Patricia Conner, Curriculum
Berryville Public Schools
Berryville, AR

Michael J. Dawkins, APPR Specialist
School Administrators Assoc of NY State
Latham, NY

Patricia L. Waller, Retired Educator
2007 President of the National Association of Biology Teachers
Allentown, PA

About the Author

Candi McKay is a national consultant and president of McKay Consulting, LLC, based in Raleigh, North Carolina. She provides customized consultation and training related to teacher quality and professional learning to school districts and state service agencies around the country. McKay works closely with teachers and school leaders at all levels to develop their capacity for ongoing reflection and professional growth.

A frequent national speaker on the topics of teacher evaluation, professional conversation, and teacher learning, Candi has also provided professional development for the nationally recognized *Framework for Teaching* for over a decade. After leaving the classroom, she began her work as a national trainer for the Educational Testing Service where she facilitated training programs associated with the *Framework for Teaching*. During this time, she also served as an adjunct faculty member at Nazareth College of Rochester, New York, where she supervised students in the Master of Science in Education degree program. As an educator and teacher leader, Candi designed and delivered professional development for teachers, participated in curriculum planning, and served as a mentor and peer coach.

McKay is a co-author of the book, *Implementing the Framework for Teaching*, an *ASCD Action Tool* (ASCD, 2009). She also developed the online professional development course, *Talk About Teaching*, based on Charlotte Danielson's book and available through Corwin and School Improvement Network.

1

Removing the Rose-Colored Glasses

Rose-colored glasses: *a cheerful or optimistic view of things,
usually without valid basis*

Dictionary.infoplease.com

The Rose-Colored Glasses Phenomenon

Gary was the principal of Washington Elementary School for thirty
years. He enjoyed his job as a school leader and maintained a congenial relationship with staff members, who described him as a kind,
caring man who always supported them. One teacher, who had frequent run-ins with parents, stated, "I can always count on Gary to go
to bat for me. He has my back." The school was one of ten schools
located in an affluent suburb that had a history of high levels of student performance. Although state assessment results at Washington
Elementary were good, they were never great. Gary's school consistently fell at the bottom of the list of elementary schools in the district

on the annual assessments of English and Language Arts. During recent years, the scores showed a gradual decline. Gary attributed the scores to a transient student demographic and the increasing class sizes due to recent budget cuts. Meanwhile, his teachers enjoyed glowing reports on their annual summative evaluations, which statistically reported 92 percent at the top or distinguished level of performance and 0 percent unsatisfactory. The remaining teachers fell in the middle.

On my first visit to Washington Elementary School, I asked Gary to show me around the school. I wanted to visit some of the classrooms and peek in on the teaching and learning that was happening. Gary wanted to set the stage for our classroom visits. "As a principal," he said, "I'm really lucky because these teachers can lead themselves. They're the best staff I've worked with in thirty years. Right now they're under a lot of pressure to perform well with the new teacher evaluation measures, and we've also been having some issues with student behavior. In spite of this, they're all doing their best. The teachers would tell you this is a great place to work."

There is an inherent comfort in seeing your environment through rose-colored glasses. All of us at some point in our lives gloss over the truth, avoiding confrontation with the brutal facts. For those responsible for leading the performance of others, there is an even stronger tendency toward this view. To explain why, let's illustrate with a few familiar examples.

Parents will measure their effectiveness by looking at the behaviors and achievements of their children. Your child gets the lead in the school play, breaks the school record for goals scored in one game, wins "student most likely to succeed," and enrolls in the Ivy League school of her choice. Who wouldn't argue that this child was raised by great parents? On the other hand, if the teacher has your number on speed dial because your child is always getting into trouble, is not completing (or finding!) his homework assignments, and is frequently described as lazy and unmotivated, you are much less likely to see yourself as a successful parent. However, many parents gloss over the facts, choosing to ignore signs that their child may be in trouble and avoid taking action to remedy the situation. Facing the truth would amount to acknowledging that they have failed in their role as parents. The reality is that many children succeed, and some will ultimately fail *in spite of their upbringing, not because of it.*

Teachers also experience the rose-colored glasses phenomenon. They measure their effectiveness through the lens of their students. As a result, many teachers are reluctant to present students with complex, challenging work which may cause their students some initial struggle and result in a lower grade. Instead, teachers will stick with a more routine, predictable path that has been tried and tested, ensuring most (if not all) students will achieve at high levels. After all, if the students are struggling and don't perform well, isn't this a sign of poor teaching? Certainly I will be seen as an exemplary teacher if most of my students attain the highest grades—even if they didn't learn anything new. Yes, the rose-colored glasses phenomenon is alive and well in many classrooms today.

Finally, principals consider themselves to be effective leaders if their teachers are performing at high levels. If 95 percent of the teachers in my building are rated "distinguished" on their annual evaluation, doesn't that say something about me as a leader? Principals, like teachers, take pride in and develop a sense of ownership of their teachers, much like a shepherd with his sheep. They watch over, protect, and guide their flock, steering clear of any danger or enemies. As a result, many principals choose to view their teachers through rose-colored glasses. I've witnessed this many times when visiting schools around the country. The building principal eagerly escorts me on a tour of the building, peeking in to classrooms along the way, showing me all of the wonderful things happening in the school–*her school*. In other words, it is difficult for anyone leading a group of people, regardless of the context, to separate the performance of those you lead from your own performance as a leader.

The presence of the rose-colored glasses phenomenon has tremendous effects on improving the quality of teaching in a school. Consider the stories of two school districts: Central Regional and Passaic Valley.

Red Flag Warnings

Central Regional School District is a district of approximately 3,000 students, nestled in a comfortable suburb in the northeast. Although they have traditionally ranked among the highest performing schools based on state assessment results, their scores have shown a gradual decline during the last three years. School district administrators attribute this decline to the constant changes made by policy makers at the State level regarding the assessments, and to having to do more with less due to budget cuts across the district.

The district is located in a state which was awarded funding for school improvement from the federal program known as Race to the Top. As a recipient of Race to the Top money, this means the district was required to make changes to their teacher evaluation process. The legislation included specific requirements regarding measures of teacher performance as well as student growth and achievement.

I was initially contacted by Tracy, the assistant superintendent for curriculum and instruction, who was familiar with the work I'd been doing to help schools make the required changes to their teacher evaluation system. Tracy wanted to know if I could send her a teacher evaluation model that would be acceptable under the new state regulations. There was an urgency in her voice that communicated this was something that needed to be taken care and checked off of her *to do* list. How soon could I send this document? Could they schedule a day of training with me next month? The district believed they could purchase a ready to go teacher evaluation model and with a day of training for the school leaders, be off and running with a new, compliant system. As I took notes during our first conversation, several red flags went up.

Much to her disappointment, I explained to the assistant superintendent that there was no *model* for teacher evaluation available for purchase. Instead, I described a process that would involve both teachers and school leaders working together to develop their own system that would accomplish several goals. First, it would promote consistency in teacher evaluation across the district by providing valid, reliable evidence about the quality of teaching. Second, it would support and encourage professional growth, with the intent to raise the quality of teaching across the district. And third, it would comply with the new state mandated regulations for teacher evaluation. Most importantly, I explained that this level of change was not an event that could be accomplished in a day. It was a process that would take time and a commitment from all stakeholders in the district.

Tracy agreed that one of the major complaints among the teaching staff was a lack of consistency in how teachers were evaluated. So the first goal made sense. But the second goal of improving teacher quality would be harder to sell. Close to 95 percent of the teachers in the district received satisfactory ratings on their annual evaluations. How would she convince them that they needed to improve and grow? Finally, she expressed doubt that she would be able to bring the teachers and administrators together to engage in this work. She described a culture of bitterness and mistrust, where teachers felt overworked, overwhelmed, and underappreciated. Even if she could get the teachers to participate in the work, they would do so with skepticism, putting up roadblocks at each step along the way. How could we move forward?

I needed to get some more information. I asked Tracy a series of questions regarding their current process for evaluating teachers and providing support to them throughout the year. What was their vision for teacher evaluations? What purpose did they serve? What criteria were their evaluations based upon? How were the evaluations conducted? Who conducted those evaluations? What procedures were in place to provide support to new teachers? What were the district's expectations for teacher performance? How good was good enough? Was this the same for all teachers? What measures were in place to identify and support struggling teachers? How was the information about the criteria, procedures, and expectations for evaluation communicated to teachers? What training was provided for school leaders or for teachers? In addition, I requested copies of any forms and procedures that were currently in use along with performance data from the three previous years of teacher evaluations.

The information supplied by the district revealed a classic case of what I call the rose-colored glasses phenomenon. Summary points follow:

• Ninety eight percent of teachers in the district received a satisfactory rating on their annual performance evaluations. This statistic remained unchanged despite the recent decline in student performance on state tests.

• Although the district had a summative evaluation form that was filled out at the end of the year, with a choice of rating teachers unsatisfactory or satisfactory, there were no definitions or agreed upon standards for what these ratings meant.

• Teacher quality was measured by means of two announced classroom observations each year for non-tenured staff members. Although tenured staff members were supposed to be evaluated each year, many had not had a formal observation in three years.

• The reports reviewed contained a "Comments" section consisting of accolades, compliments, and expressions of gratitude for "being a valued member of our school community." None of the reports included any evidence of student performance or suggestions for teacher growth.

• When leaders were asked what characteristics they would use to define *effective practice*, there was no agreement or consistency in their responses.

• When teachers were asked to state the criteria for attaining a satisfactory rating, their responses varied. "It depends on who's looking." "To be honest, I can't tell you." "A well behaved, compliant classroom. That's the ticket." "Criteria? I didn't know there were any criteria! I show up, do my job, and know what my evaluation will say."

Rather than accept the reality that the district was in decline and the teachers were on a sinking ship, the school leaders chose to wear rose-colored glasses, avoiding any mention of improvement needed. Apparently this was easier than challenging the status quo. Unless the school leaders were able to remove their rose-colored glasses, moving forward would be difficult, if not impossible.

Demonstrating Moral Courage

The story of Passaic Valley Schools demonstrates how a school district can improve the quality of teaching by recognizing and confronting the rose-colored glasses phenomenon, replacing it with transparency in their interactions with one another. Passaic Valley is a school district that understands the connections between instructional leadership, teacher quality, and student achievement. A district with fourteen schools and close to 10,000 students, Passaic Valley began their journey with a vision of continuous learning for all based on a set of core beliefs and a commitment to action. Translated, this meant involving stakeholders from all levels across the district, from teaching assistants right up to the superintendent's office. This group of stakeholders was formed shortly after the State Education Department labeled Passaic Valley a "district in need of improvement." Two of the district's fourteen schools had failed to make adequate yearly progress (AYP) for students two years in a row.

Armed with recent research demonstrating the impact teacher quality has on student learning, the committee set its first priority to examine the district's process for measuring teaching performance. They collected student achievement data and teacher evaluation reports from all fourteen schools. What they found was startling. Regardless of student achievement results, teachers in every school across the district were consistently given satisfactory ratings. The evaluations demonstrated another case of the rose-colored glasses phenomenon.

However, unlike Central Regional School District, Passaic Valley was able to move forward because their leaders were driven by *moral courage*, the essential condition needed for school leaders to improve the quality of teaching and student learning. Not only must school leaders recognize the need for change, they must be willing to make the change happen. Moral courage is what enables leaders to challenge the status quo and face the inevitable tension that comes from rocking the boat. Ultimately moral courage is doing whatever it takes to put students first. Without this essential attribute, there is little chance of making the changes needed to impact teaching and learning.

The Passaic Valley committee spent the next year redesigning their teacher evaluation system, creating a process based on evidence of teaching and learning that was transparent to all. In addition to the development of new forms and procedures, their plan included training and support for teachers and school leaders. The design and implementation of this change occurred over several years, involving hard work that was both emotionally and intellectually demanding for all. This process and the steps they took are described in subsequent chapters.

Leading Change: Necessary Dispositions

What are the guiding principles and predispositions of principals who are able to remove their rose-colored glasses to create and sustain improvements in teaching? This question must be addressed if we are to improve the quality of teaching. The answer extends beyond leadership training programs or professional development opportunities. School leaders attend hours, days, and even week long training sessions related to instructional practice for the purpose of enhancing teaching in their buildings. However, even the most comprehensive professional development plan for engaging leaders in training; one that provides opportunities to practice the skills of supervision, coaching, and teacher evaluation; provides no guarantee of improvements in teaching. This is one of the greatest challenges (and frustrations) to those of us in a consulting role. Consultants are limited in their ability to effect lasting change. Change does not occur during periodic visits to a school. It happens when teachers and school leaders make a commitment to implement the change and apply what they've learned.

Learning the *what* and *how* of effective instruction will not improve the quality of teaching unless school leaders possess certain habits of mind that enable them to engage teachers in meaningful learning. Improving teacher quality begins with school leadership. Schmoker (2006) states "It's this simple: schools won't improve until the average building leader begins to work cooperatively with teachers to truly, meaningfully oversee and improve instructional quality" (p. 29). What are the traits of school leaders who make learning for all the top priority of the school and are able to communicate and realize this vision—a clear vision without rose-colored glasses?

Perceptions About the Role of a School Leader

Why is it that some school leaders are often found out and about, visiting classrooms, talking with teachers, tracking down resources for professional development, or engaged in collegial circles and study groups with teachers? Is it because they have less responsibility than their colleagues? Have they found more time in the school day? Did they discover extra money in the school budget to hire someone to handle discipline? How do they manage to spend so much time focusing on instruction?

The way that school leaders perceive their role has tremendous impact on how their time is allocated each day. Am I a competent building manager, one who engages in good public relations? A master scheduler, one who ensures that every minute of the school day is carefully planned for teachers and students? Do I regard my role as an authoritarian figure, whose responsibility is to communicate and impose state and local mandates for program and curriculum changes, new standards for teacher accountability, or the teaching of twenty-first century skills? Or, do I believe that my primary role is to grow and support the quality of teaching to improve opportunities for student learning?

Before school leaders can begin to think about how to improve teacher quality, they must first question their purpose as a school leader. Charlotte Danielson writes in her book, *Talk About Teaching* (2009), that leaders must understand their role as leader in a professional organization and be able to clearly communicate their vision for professional learning," . . . an essential characteristic of leadership is to paint a compelling picture of what schools can accomplish and why it is important to do so" (p. 22).

Visionary leaders, Danielson writes, are able convey to teachers a larger sense of purpose that motivates ordinary people to extraordinary accomplishments. And they are able to inspire others to recognize their place in that vision.

What we know is that many principals view themselves as managers first, with instructional leadership taking a back seat. One explanation for this may be the fact that many current school leaders stepped into their positions during a time when their role was defined in terms of school-based management. In a paper written by Richard Elmore (2000) for the Albert Shanker Institute, he eloquently describes how school leaders were seen just one short decade ago:

> Administration in education, then, has come to mean not the management of instruction but the management of the structures and processes around instruction. School leaders are hired and retained based largely on their capacity to buffer teachers from outside interference and their capacity to support the prevailing logic of confidence between a school system and its constituencies. (p. 6–7)

More recently, researchers at Stanford University confirmed that principals allocate scant time in the service of teaching and learning. The study examined how principals spend their time during the school day. Organizing their daily tasks into six categories, researchers found that *principals devote the least amount of their total day to instruction-related activities.* The research showed that on average, principals spend less than 6 percent of the school day in classrooms. Of that 6 percent, less than 1 percent of that time was spent providing instructional feedback to improve teaching (Horng, Klasik, & Loeb, 2009). Fink and Resnick (2001) offer further evidence of this. Their research showed that," . . . in practice few principals act as genuine instructional leaders. Most principals spend relatively little time in classrooms and even less time analyzing instruction with teachers" (p. 598).

While there are many reasons principals cite for giving less emphasis to instructional leadership (lack of time ranks highest), I believe that the principals' perception about their role as a leader is one of the essential principles that determine how they spend their day. A school leader must believe that they have *no greater role* than improving the quality of teaching in their school. If we agree that the quality of teaching is the single most important factor that impacts student learning, then we must also agree that improving the quality of teaching is the single most important role of a school leader. For this belief to be realized, leaders must recognize that even the best teachers need to continue to learn and grow. We've established that teaching is really hard, complex work. It's been said that few people do more thinking on their feet than teachers who are faced with making split second decisions that have lasting consequences. It is no criticism to say that all teachers have room for improvement.

Yet when visiting schools around the country, I meet principals who at the very suggestion that teachers be asked to explain events observed in their classrooms or suggest a different approach or strategy, jump to their defense. "These teachers are working very hard. They have made tremendous improvements in their practice. They have a lot of pressure on them, and they're really doing their best. They trust me and I would never want to jeopardize the relationship I have with them by questioning their teaching." These words (or some variation thereof) are spoken with much frequency.

Let's get one thing straight. Teaching is complex, difficult work, requiring ongoing learning and growth. Even the best among us have room for improvement. This is the reality of teaching. Improving the quality of teaching begins with a school leader who makes it a priority to regularly visit classrooms, engage teachers in professional conversations, and provide frequent opportunities for teachers to collaborate and engage in collegial discussion. With all of the demands of school leadership—the meetings, deadlines, paperwork, phone calls, troubleshooting with parents, school custodians, bus drivers . . . the list is endless—*how do leaders find the time* to improve the quality of teaching? By believing there is no greater role than to do so.

There are still many principals who acknowledge the importance of their role as an instructional leader, yet they report spending less time in classrooms observing teaching and providing feedback to teachers about instruction than they believe is necessary. What are some of the other factors that drive successful school leaders to engage in practices that promote teacher learning? Why is it that some principals find the time to lead the learning in their schools while for others, professional conversations about teaching and learning are but a rare occurrence?

Confidence in Self as an Instructional Leader

In a recent article written for the Harvard Education Letter, Thomas Fowler-Finn described what it takes to be an effective instructional leader (Walser, 2011). In an interview conducted by Nancy Walser, Fowler stated:

> The main challenge is that principals, *especially veterans*, lack a working knowledge and confidence in the role of instructional leadership. . . . The requirements on veterans are to do a job for which they were not prepared, educated, or hired. The circumstances aren't that much different for the newly hired. (p. 6, [italics added])

With expectations for school leaders continually being reshaped and their positions under endless scrutiny and attack, it is no wonder that many school leaders question themselves, wondering if they will be able to fill the shoes of the twenty-first century leader (as it continues to be defined). And yet, in spite of this ever changing climate of increasing expectations and public scrutiny, we find leaders who are able to move their teachers forward, creating and sustaining a culture of high expectations and professional learning. These leaders exude confidence in their role in leading the learning.

There are many factors that shape the confidence of a school leader. Was I a teacher before becoming a school leader? A successful teacher who loved to learn? Or, was teaching a puzzle that presented me with more questions than answers? Did the leadership program I attended adequately prepare me to evaluate the quality of teaching? Do I understand the principles of learning and how it occurs? Am I able to provide specific feedback about instructional practice? Do central office personnel respect and support my work?

While school leaders come from diverse backgrounds, successful school leaders have demonstrated instructional leadership experience both as teachers and as valued members of their school communities. Leaders who transition from successful teaching experiences to school leadership bring a level of confidence to their new role that may not exist for some of their colleagues. Confidence that results from success in teaching propels leaders to establish high standards for instructional practice in their schools. Leaders who understand the challenges of teaching and were able to successfully navigate through this complex territory are more likely and better able to engage teachers in meaningful learning. They recognize the importance of providing teachers with the resources that will improve and accelerate learning. Having experienced success themselves, they are motivated to take on the role of an instructional leader. Success breeds confidence. Confidence becomes their motivator.

A Growth Mindset

Leaders who fail to grow, learn, and improve are doomed to failure. We frequently talk about the demands of teaching, that it is really hard, intellectual work. It requires teachers to continually reflect on practice and to seek new and more effective ways to help students learn. Successful instructional leaders seek opportunities to grow alongside the teachers. Chapters Three and Four make explicit that what leaders and teachers need to know are essentially the same. So when we talk about teacher learning, we include leaders in that learning as well. Much as is the case for teachers, school leaders need to constantly adapt, change, and grow in the face of ever increasing demands of their work. Essentially, you can't lead what you don't know.

Carol Dweck's fascinating book, *Mindset* (2006), describes two different perspectives on the way people view intelligence that have direct relevance to school leadership. This view, she writes, has a profound effect on the way you lead your life (and ultimately, the way you lead others). Those who believe they are born with a certain dose of intelligence that does not, cannot, and will not change over time possess what Dweck calls a *fixed mindset*. A *growth mindset*, on the other hand, is based on the belief that the intelligence you were born with is just a starting point, that intelligence can grow and be cultivated over time through your efforts and experiences.

Leaders with a fixed mindset limit their ability to learn, grow, and achieve because they are consumed with proving themselves, worried more about having their intelligence validated based on their actions.

They judge themselves and others based on how they succeed or fail in every situation. This view can paralyze even the most intelligent and talented leaders because they fear that if they fail, their intelligence will be questioned. Leaders with a fixed mindset shrink away from challenges that require effort. For them, the need to expend effort signals a lack of intelligence or talent. After all, if you were smart, this task wouldn't be so hard, right? In addition, those with a fixed mindset don't respond well to criticism. They fear feedback that may suggest improvement is needed. They believe their potential is carved in stone, a permanent state. Don't ask me to step up or improve. What you see is what you get. It is what it is.

On the other hand, in the world of the growth mindset, effort is what makes you smart or talented. Failure is just a necessary precursor to learning and growth. People with a growth mindset don't just seek challenge, they thrive on it. The bigger the challenge, the more they stretch. They seek constructive criticism because, unlike their fixed mindset counterparts, feedback is regarded as a conduit to growth rather than an indictment of their lack of ability. Leaders who operate with a growth mindset have a passion for learning. They value the learning experiences and persevere when the going gets tough because they believe this is the best way to cultivate and grow their abilities. No limits, no boundaries.

How does mindset impact instructional leadership? Michael Fullan writes in *The Moral Imperative of School Leadership*, "Tools are only as effective as the mindset that guides their use" (2003, p. 68). School leaders with a growth mindset are easy to spot in a professional development session. Much of the work we do with school leaders involves challenging prevailing beliefs and changing habits that have been ingrained for a very long time. Leaders who have a growth mindset are comfortable with the tension that is created when we are learning and practicing new skills. They understand that there are no quick fixes and that change is the result of repetition and practice over time. They respond to the challenges presented to them in training with optimism and enthusiasm. They see learning as an opportunity to improve their skills and enable them to better promote professional learning among their staff. Leaders with a growth mindset will implement the skills they've acquired to make changes that will improve the quality of teaching, even if they are initially met with resistance from teachers. Why? Because leaders with a growth mindset have the expectation that all teachers can learn, grow, and improve practice. They provide opportunities for teachers to engage in rigorous work and provide constructive feedback to them along the way. Growth mindset leaders seek out opportunities to talk to teachers about instruction, for they see this as a way for leaders themselves to learn and grow. Leaders who operate with a growth mindset have a contagious passion for learning that teachers quickly recognize. As a result, teachers in this environment are more willing take risks that learning and growth require because they know they have the support and understanding of their leader.

Moral Courage

When I think of all the traits of school leaders that contribute to improving teacher quality, I believe that moral courage is the single most important trait, yet the most overlooked in literature about school leadership. Moral courage is what enables us to act when we know that in doing so, we may jeopardize how we are viewed by others either personally or professionally. Our actions are driven by our values, what we believe is the right thing to do or say, regardless of how we may be received or regarded by others. I've seen many acts of moral courage demonstrated by educators and leaders from all levels:

- A teacher who publicly defends a new teacher evaluation process that has the potential to expose marginal teaching because she believes it will result in improved instruction and better opportunities for students

- A principal who calls out a veteran teacher who uses inappropriate language with high school students to gain their acceptance and friendship

- A director of human resources who hires the more qualified teacher candidate from outside the district over a substitute teacher who has been recommended and is liked by other staff members

- An assistant superintendent who questions principals about inconsistencies in the procedures they are using to evaluate and report teacher performance across the district

- A principal who, based on solid evidence collected using multiple measures, rates a veteran teacher unsatisfactory on an annual evaluation of performance

- An athletic coach who reports that his star player has failed to meet academic eligibility requirements, thereby removing the player from participating in the championship game

- A board of education member who votes to terminate the employment of a popular teacher based on the recommendation and evidence presented by the superintendent despite threats from community members

- A teacher who volunteers to allow principals to conduct practice observations in his classroom despite recommendations from the union that doing so will set an unwanted precedent

- A principal who challenges the decision of the superintendent to make teacher attendance at monthly faculty meetings optional as a concession for teachers agreeing to one less planning period per month in their schedules

- A new principal who participates in a paired observation recognizes inconsistencies and bias in the ratings awarded to a popular teacher by a veteran colleague and questions the ratings

School leadership will not impact teaching without leaders who demonstrate moral courage. Moral courage is most likely to make an appearance if a leader has the qualities previously discussed: a belief that his first role is to improve teaching and learning, confidence in ability to lead the learning, and a mindset that we all have the potential to grow and learn when we engage in rigorous and challenging work.

Without moral courage, no amount of training or learning experiences will yield changes in the quality of teaching and learning. The experiences described at Passaic Valley Schools earlier in this chapter illustrate what happens when leaders demonstrate moral courage. Training and leadership preparation programs enable leaders to recognize the need for change. In subsequent chapters, we'll describe, in detail, what leaders need to know and understand so they are able to recognize effective teaching practices, and know when to signal the need for change.

Moral courage is what empowers leaders to move from knowing to doing. It enables them to apply their understandings about teaching and learning to make the changes needed to improve the quality of teaching.

Key Points About Removing the Rose-Colored Glasses

The first and most essential step to improving the quality of teaching is for leaders to remove their rose-colored glasses and really *see* teaching for what it is. School leaders who have successfully disposed of their rose-colored glasses (or perhaps never owned any) possess certain qualities or traits that enable them to lead with honesty, integrity, and consistency. They act with moral courage that empowers them to put students first, regardless of how they may be viewed by colleagues, teachers, students, or the community at large.

To display moral courage requires certain dispositions or habits of mind on the part of school leaders. Successful leaders have a vision for their school that is driven by their understanding of learning and the importance of having a qualified teacher in every classroom. They believe their primary role is that of an instructional leader rather than a school-based manager. They make instructional quality the top priority of the school and are able to help teachers recognize their role in that vision.

School leaders who exhibit moral courage are confident in the role of instructional leadership. They understand the complexity of teaching and the need for ongoing learning. Many were once teachers themselves, and they recognize the importance of providing teachers with the time and resources needed to continually meet the ever changing demands of the profession.

Another predisposition successful school leaders have is a growth mindset. Leaders who are driven by a growth mindset seek opportunities to learn and grow and expect teachers to do the same. They are not discouraged by failure, criticism, or challenge; they believe that it is through these experiences that one grows and improves. Where others see despair, leaders with a growth mindset see hope and promise. They see potential in every teacher and in every student. This mindset is what propels them toward moral courage. They are willing to speak out, take a risk, and challenge conventional wisdom, knowing they may face criticism or failure.

The rose-colored glasses phenomenon has created a sense of complacency in many schools where all of the teaching is satisfactory and instructional practice is never challenged. How do school leaders engage teachers in the change process needed to improve the quality of teaching? In the next chapter, we'll look at how successful leaders apply these habits of mind to implement change in their schools and create a culture for learning.

Putting Words Into Action

Reflecting on Your Current State

- How do you view the quality of teaching in your building? What evidence would you use to support this view?

- What are some recent examples of how you've demonstrated moral courage in your role as an instructional leader?

Action Tools

- How Do You Spend Your Day?

  - Use Table 1.1: Daily Tracker for three days during the same week. What portion of your day is spent in the service of instructional leadership? What will you keep doing? What will you change?

- Gap Analysis

  - Respond to the Teacher Evaluation Survey in Figure 1.1.

  - Ask teachers to complete the survey.

  - Tally the teacher scores for each survey item and determine an average score.

  - Determine the gap between your scores and the average teacher score. What conclusions can you draw? Do teachers share your view about teacher evaluation and professional growth?

Table 1.1   Daily Tracker

Date _____

Time: START - STOP	Total Time	DESCRIPTION	I (Instructional) M (Managerial) O (Other)

Figure 1.1   Teacher Evaluation Survey

Directions: Rate the following statements about teacher evaluation on a four-point scale:

Strongly Disagree	Somewhat Disagree	Somewhat Agree	Strongly Agree
1	2	3	4

General Questions About Teacher Evaluation

1 2 3 4   Research-based teacher evaluation can improve teaching.

1 2 3 4   Research-based teacher evaluation, done right, can improve student learning.

1 2 3 4   Administrators can be trained to conduct evaluations properly.

1 2 3 4   I know what research says about the qualities of teaching that impact student learning.

1 2 3 4   I know what research says about teacher evaluation.

1 2 3 4   Teachers have information to add to the observation that makes their evaluation more accurate.

1 2 3 4   Teacher evaluation systems can be improved to make them more valuable.

1 2 3 4   Time invested in properly evaluating teachers is worth it.

Information About Evaluation in This District

1 2 3 4   Administrators in my district are qualified to evaluate teachers.

1 2 3 4   Administrators in my building are qualified to evaluate teachers.

1 2 3 4   The items upon which teachers are currently being evaluated are based on research.

1 2 3 4   Teacher evaluation in my district is fair.

1 2 3 4   Teacher evaluation in my district is rigorous and reveals what is true about teachers' practices.

1 2 3 4   Teacher evaluation in my district is confidential.

1 2 3 4   Teacher evaluation in my district is respectfully conducted.

1 2 3 4   Teacher evaluation in my district is based upon collected facts, not opinion.

1 2 3 4   Teacher input is an important part of teacher evaluation in my district.

1 2 3 4   Teacher evaluation is currently being done properly in my district.

1 2 3 4   Teacher evaluation is valued in my district.

1 2 3 4   Teacher evaluation is currently used to improve teaching in my district

1 2 3 4   Teachers in this district want to continuously improve their practice.

1 2 3 4   Teacher evaluation plays a role in helping teachers improve their practice in this district.

1 2 3 4   Administrators in this district support the continuous improvement of teaching.

Please use this space to make any additional comments on current teacher evaluation practices in your district/building:

2

No More Lake Wobegon

Creating a Culture of Learning

It's what you learn after you know it all that counts.

John Wooden

The Effects of Well-Intended Fiction: A Culture of Nice

The relationship between teacher quality and student learning is clear. Effective teachers significantly influence student achievement. A growing body of research finds teaching to be the single most important school-based factor impacting student performance. When we combine this fact with the current statistics that indicate most teachers in this country receive satisfactory evaluation ratings, one might conclude that student achievement is soaring. And yet, we don't have to look far to find statistics that reveal a growing gap in the knowledge and skills students need to compete in the global economy of the twenty-first century. In his book *Results Now* (2006), Mike Schmoker described the "shock and awe" he experienced visiting classrooms. I share one of the most striking studies from Schmoker's book:

In 2005, Learning 24/7 conducted a study based on 1,500 class-room observations. Their findings:

- 4% Classrooms in which there was evidence of a clear learning objective
- 3% Classrooms in which there was evidence of higher order thinking
- 0% Classrooms in which students were either writing or using rubrics
- 85% Classrooms in which fewer than one half of students were paying attention
- 52% Classrooms in which students were using worksheets
- 35% Classrooms in which non-instructional activities were occurring (p. 18)

Despite an increasing number of similar studies that demonstrate a growing achievement gap, teacher evaluation statistics remain unchanged. Teacher evaluation systems fail to reliably assess teacher performance. Instead of capturing the variation in teacher effectiveness that one would expect to see in *any* school system, most teachers fall into the same category, satisfactory or above. From the report issued by the Center for American Progress, *So Long, Lake Wobegon?* (Donaldson, 2009), they revealed that:

- Over four years, nearly 100 percent of Chicago teachers were rated "satisfactory" or above.
- Ninety-six percent of San Bernardino, CA's teachers met or exceeded expectations for the 2002–03 and 2003–04 school years.
- Between 1995 and 2005 only 1 in every 930 teachers (.1 percent) in Illinois received an unsatisfactory rating.
- Ninety-nine percent of Oregon teachers are rated satisfactory each year. (p. 9)

I've read hundreds of reports completed by school leaders from all over the country. Many teacher evaluation reports today represent nothing more than a well-intended fiction. Satisfactory ratings are given in the absence of any evidence to support them. Accolades to the teacher abound and, in rare instances, a few suggestions for improvement are noted. In one district where we reviewed over one hundred reports, the field for evidence on the report read "No comments." Next to "No comments" was a rating of "Effective," or "Highly Effective."

I'm sure some would argue that the amount of time these reports consume is a contributing factor. They believe there simply isn't enough time to collect and provide evidence to support all of the ratings for every teacher and, besides that, they tell me, "I know these teachers are doing a great job." Although there are a number of factors that contribute to the lack of consistency, validity, and reliability of evaluation reports, I believe that what we're witnessing is yet another effect of the rose-colored glasses phenomenon described in Chapter One.

As a result, many school environments today suffer from what Garrison Keillor referred to as the "Lake Wobegon" effect, where most if not all teaching is rated above average. This has tremendous impact on how teachers regard opportunities for professional learning aimed at improving practice. When overall teacher performance is rated satisfactory (or better), it presents a challenge to school leaders to create a culture where improving teacher quality is valued. After all, if it's not broken, why fix it?

The Changing Landscape

Experts and education leaders have increasingly come to see current teacher evaluation methods as inadequate, largely because they fail to differentiate between teachers with varying levels of effectiveness. Recognizing the importance of teacher quality to student learning, policymakers at the local, state, and federal levels are now focusing on new measures of teacher effectiveness, aimed at improving teacher performance. From the Department of Education's Race to the Top initiative that urges states and districts to use measures of student growth as part of a teacher performance evaluation to the District of Columbia's IMPACT system that led both to significant bonuses for high performing teachers and the dismissal of low performing teachers, there is an increasing demand for more transparent and accurate methods to quantify teacher performance. These new programs aimed at improving the quality of teaching will change the landscape of Lake Wobegon.

A central principle of the Race to the Top criteria is that states need viable approaches to measure the effectiveness of teaching, provide a rating to each individual teacher, and use those ratings to inform professional development, compensation, promotion, tenure, and dismissal. A state's approach must include multiple measures, including measures of student growth. Other measures must be used in ratings of teacher effectiveness, such as structured observations of teachers, review of teacher portfolios, and assessments of teacher competencies, knowledge, and skills.

What does this mean for the teachers of Lake Wobegon and beyond? Simply stated, it means that teacher ratings will change. Teachers who have become accustomed to receiving the highest rating each year (usually this is "satisfactory"), may no longer achieve the highest score. The lens through which we examine the quality of teaching has changed. It includes a much more comprehensive look at teaching than we have settled for in the past, with research-based standards and levels of performance that raise the bar across the board. As a result of this new lens, the landscape of teacher effectiveness will also change. Teachers and school leaders will have greater opportunities for constructive feedback about teaching and learning, focused on specific components of practice.

How can school leaders help teachers change existing mindsets that fear constructive criticism and feedback to mindsets that create school environments where professional learning for all is an expectation and teachers understand that you don't have to be bad to get better? This chapter will describe the process of implementing this change beginning with the leader's role in setting the stage for moving the staff forward. Just as there are certain qualities that enable leaders to remove their rose-colored glasses and view teaching through a clear, objective lens, leaders who are able to cultivate the ground and ready it for change approach this task armed with a set of beliefs and understandings about learning.

The Leader's Role: Essential Beliefs and Understandings

Changing Beliefs: Practice Comes First!

We all make choices about how to allocate our time. Most of us tend to spend more time in places and to do things that we are comfortable with, enjoy, or that have given us the greatest level of satisfaction in the past. Conversely, we tend to avoid or put off those tasks that appear overwhelming, stressful, or unpleasant. Leaders who bring successful teaching experiences to their role are more likely to be found in classrooms and engaged in professional conversations with teachers. This is where they are most comfortable and have seen the greatest impact in learning. They don't wait for an opportune moment to visit a classroom to listen in on what students are learning or to talk with a teacher about that teacher's success implementing the new math series. They just do it.

There are, of course, other leaders who bring little or no teaching experience to their position. Or, they may have entered their administrative role without having had much success in the classroom. They may not recognize the connection between effective practice and student learning, because they've never experienced the *aha moments* students have when learning happens. These leaders may be really great at developing a master schedule or finding extra money in the school budget to hire extra staff, but when it comes to instruction and learning they are more comfortable delegating those responsibilities to others, giving them time to stick with what they know and do well. What we need are leaders (and teachers) who believe that student learning is the single most important responsibility of teachers and that improving the quality of teaching is the most important role of school leadership.

How do we begin to change beliefs about what is most important? When the new process is unfamiliar, questions past practices, or pushes at the margins of existing skills sets, believing in the value of change presents a challenge. Even when school leaders themselves are committed to providing opportunities for teacher learning, changing existing mindsets and norms can be very difficult. All school leaders have experienced the power of prevailing cultures to undermine change efforts. I recall being asked by a veteran teacher, "Why are we being asked to develop goals for professional learning when no one has ever said there is anything wrong with our teaching?"

As Doug Reeves (2007), renowned author and expert in the field of leadership and learning states, "To challenge that culture, school leaders must be prepared to stand up for effective practice even if changes are initially unpopular.... Change inevitably represents risk, loss, and fear, a triumvirate never associated with popularity" (p. 86). Although conventional wisdom is that beliefs drive our behavior, a number of respected educators and researchers challenge this perspective. Tom Guskey (1999) presents a model for change that demonstrates the power of experience in shaping beliefs:

> The crucial point is that it is not the professional development *per se*, but the experience of successful implementation that changes teachers' attitudes and beliefs. They believe it works because they have seen it work, and that experience shapes their attitudes and beliefs . . . the key element in significant change in teachers' attitudes and beliefs is clear evidence of improvement in the learning outcomes of their students. (p. 384)

During one of my years as a classroom teacher, I had an inclusion class with twenty-seven fifth graders, six of whom had been identified with learning disabilities. As a result, there was a teaching assistant assigned to my room whose role was to provide instructional support throughout the day. At the time, the district was having difficulty filling daily requests for substitute teachers, so they would frequently send the teaching assistant to classrooms where they needed coverage. This frequently left me on my own to manage a very needy group of students. Although it presented a great challenge, it turned into one of the most valuable learning experiences that changed my beliefs, and ultimately my practice. During this period of time, I learned that these fifth graders were more capable than I ever imagined of taking responsibility for their learning. Without an assistant to help out, I quickly realized that I would need the students to step up and indeed they did. With a few new structures and routines in place, students began to rely on each other for help, asking questions when they would get stuck, pairing up to complete a task, and even designing a list of work they could do independently while waiting for help from the teacher. It was amazing, and it changed my beliefs about my role as a teacher. The more I expected of the students, the more they would take on. The students were willing participants in this change, confessing they liked having additional responsibility and choice in their learning.

When it comes to change, experience and practice win out every time. Richard Elmore (2010) has made the same observation:

> Resilient, powerful new beliefs—the kinds of beliefs that transform the way we think about how children are treated in schools, for example—are shaped by people engaging in behaviors or practices that are deeply unfamiliar to them and that test the outer limits of their knowledge, their confidence in themselves as practitioners, and their competencies. (p. 2)

This has tremendous implications for both teachers as well as school leaders. In his article "What Can We Do About Teacher Resistance?" Jim Knight (2009) states, "When it comes to change, teachers have to drink the water, so to speak, before they will believe" (p. 510).

Drinking the Water

One of the best ways to give school leaders and teachers an opportunity to "drink the water" is by participating in short, brief classroom visits that are followed by a professional conversation between the leader and teacher. Without any strings of evaluation attached, leaders can spend ten minutes in a teacher's classroom, and they will have seen and heard enough about teaching and learning to be able to engage that teacher in a meaningful conversation about practice. These visits can also occur among teachers, when they visit each other's classrooms and then have an opportunity to talk, reflect, ask questions, and engage in professional learning. Once teachers and leaders experience the benefit of these visits, their beliefs and attitudes about classroom observations and the conversations that follow begin to change. They will view these visits as learning opportunities, rather than a chance to get raked over the coals.

I frequently visit classrooms around the country for the purpose of helping teachers and school leaders develop the skills needed for these visits to be meaningful and productive. I will never forget the response a high school physics teacher had after a brief visit to an English teacher's classroom on one of my visits to a high school in a suburb of Rochester, New York. The physics teacher was so inspired to see the strategies used by her colleague in the English department that she was hardly able to sit still in her seat during our debrief session to discuss the lesson. She couldn't wait to follow up with her colleague to learn more about how he set up the learning activity with his students so successfully!

These brief classroom visits are just one example of how practice drives beliefs. School leaders will be more successful in leading change that improves teaching when they provide teachers with opportunities to experience the benefits of changing practice. Reeves (2009) validates the importance of providing teachers with frequent opportunities to recognize effective practice. He calls them "short-term wins" explaining that effective leaders create short-term wins by designing plans for teachers to receive immediate feedback to reinforce effective practice and modify ineffective practice. Without short-term wins, he says, "the pain of change often overwhelms the anticipated long-term benefits" (p. 92). To experienced educators, this concept is nothing new. It's exactly what we strive for by providing students with formative feedback throughout their learning experiences. Meaningful feedback is a powerful motivator and a critical, but often underused, tool for improving professional practice and student learning.

One of the greatest challenges for school leaders is to engage in what Blanchard, Meyer, and Ruhe (2007) call, "spaced repetition," or practice, spaced out over time:

It is difficult to change a belief, send a voter to the ballot box, or influence a person to contribute to charity through one interaction. We do not make people see, feel, or do something in one sentence. An important message almost always requires repetition over time if it's going to have its intended result. (p. 14)

Understanding About Learning

Successful school leaders help teachers change their beliefs about learning. But how does teacher learning and growth occur? A school leader's answer to this question has serious implications on the success of lasting improvements in teaching. Successful school leaders understand learning and how it occurs, and are able to apply their understanding to teacher learning.

In his book, *Thinking for a Living: How to Get Better Performance and Results from Knowledge Workers*, Thomas Davenport (2005) uses a term for those who think for a living. "Knowledge workers," he calls them, like autonomy. He explains that, "thinking for a living engenders thinking for oneself. Knowledge workers are paid for their education, experience and expertise, so it is not surprising that they take offense when someone else rides roughshod over their intellectual territory" (p. 15). If we consider teaching to be a thinking person's job (as it most surely is), we can apply this need for autonomy to teacher learning and growth. A school leader who ignores this need, depriving teachers of any choice or input, insisting that all teachers attend the same one size fits all training, and requiring them to implement the same instructional strategies without any regard for their relevance or applicability, creates push back and resentment from teachers, not improvement and growth.

Respecting the need for teacher autonomy, however, does not mean that teachers are not accountable to clear standards of practice. A leader who is successful in gaining teacher support for change and growth is one who is able to balance the teacher's need for autonomy within a research-based framework for effective practice. That is, teacher autonomy is supported within the boundaries of agreed upon standards of professional practice.

To create a mindset for change, then, school leaders need to believe that teacher learning occurs when the learner is given the opportunity to do the thinking, to create, develop, and make choices that are meaningful and impactful. Designs for teacher learning that are one size fits all, top down, or "drive by" sessions with no meaning or relevancy will not engender support or buy in from any professional staff. This concept about learning and how it occurs not only applies to teacher learning, it's about *learning, period.* A school leader needs to approach teacher learning and growth based on this very simple understanding.

A Presumption of Continuous Growth for All

People rise to high expectations when those they respect have confidence that they will.

John Goodlad (in Fullan, 2003, p. xi)

The success of a school leader to create a mindset where change, improvement, and continuous growth are the norm is also dependent on how the leader views the instructional capacity of his or her staff. We mentioned earlier that there are many leaders who characterize their staff as being highly skilled, experienced, and dedicated professionals. Do these same leaders also believe their teachers are capable of further growth and development? Is there a presumption of continuous growth and improvement for all teachers? Or are teachers in these schools complacent about their own growth because they demonstrated their competency years ago ("I have tenure, you know!"), and the notion of change or improvement would only signal trouble?

There are, of course, leaders who accept status quo and sidestep their role of improving teacher quality because they lack confidence in their teachers as instructional specialists. These are the leaders who will tell me, "They're really doing the best they can with the students they're given to teach. We can't expect any more from them." Or, leaders may demonstrate what we refer to as leniency with teachers who are great to have around, but may not be contributing much to student learning. "Tom is such a nice guy. He's a real favorite among students and parents." Or, "I can always rely on Heather when I need a volunteer or someone to organize the holiday parties."

To improve the quality of teaching, leaders must believe in the competence and instructional capacity of their staff, and that staff members are *able to learn and grow.* More importantly, leaders must demonstrate through words and deeds an expectation of continuous learning for *all.* We don't accept the notion that some of our students can't learn. We expect continuous learning of all students. Given the complexity and demands of teaching, why would we expect any less from our teachers?

Successful school leaders, able to lead change that improves the quality of teaching, possess certain beliefs and understandings that make creating the culture of learning possible. Rather than try to convince teachers of the value of change and growth, successful leaders provide teachers with opportunities for short-term wins, enabling them to experience through practice and periodic feedback, the benefits of effective change. Leaders must also understand that learning happens when teachers are involved in doing the mental work, creating and developing ideas and strategies that are meaningful and relevant. Finally, teacher learning and growth occur in an environment that expects continuous learning and growth for all. You don't have to be bad to get better!

Setting the Stage: Defining Who We Are

Capturing the School's History

Creating the culture and establishing norms for teacher learning is the first step to improving teacher quality. What are some of the actions leaders can take to engage teachers in this culture of learning? One of the most important steps in leading change is to acknowledge and honor the contributions and experiences of the past. We've all experienced times when various stakeholders express feelings of "we've been there, done that" or bring skepticism or ill will to the initiative because of similar experiences they've had in the past that didn't turn out so well.

In their book, *Building Shared Responsibility for Student Learning*, Anne Conzemius and Jan O'Neill (2001) describe a process for moving forward while honoring the past. Whenever I begin working with a new school or district, it is always based on the assumption that there are no blank slates, that we are not starting from scratch. No matter what the current state of affairs may be when changes are initiated, there are always practices, strategies, and traditions that are worth keeping. The "Historygram" process of Conzemius and O'Neill (2001, p. 29) is one that I've used many times when working with faculties about to embark on a new initiative, as a tool to build a bridge between the past and the future. It gives everyone in the school community an opportunity to reflect together in order to learn about the history of the school. The process evolves as a timeline that builds the organizational history through stories that are told by members of the school community beginning with the *tribal elders* and ending with the newly hired. Teachers learn about one another and begin to understand and respect differing points of view as they listen to their colleagues tell stories about past initiatives, major turning points, successes, and crises. This process helps build a new vision that everyone can share.

There are many ways to create an opportunity for staff members to share the school history. We typically begin by asking the entire group to form a line around the room's perimeter based on the order in which they joined the staff, beginning with the longest standing member. Once the line is formed, we divide the staff into groups based on an era or span of years when they were hired. The chart in Figure 2.1 demonstrates what a sample distribution might look like once teachers were put into groups.

Each group is given a story board or chart paper and asked to name their era. The groups are asked to capture this moment in time by illustrating the storyboard. Guidelines for what to include might be

- Major events or initiatives (capital funds project, the arrival of new technology, changes in school structure or scheduling)
- What was happening in the community
- What was happening in the world
- Traditions, ceremonies, and celebrations that occurred
- What worked: values they want to take into the future

Each group designates a "historian" to describe the contents of the storyboard. After all groups have shared, the entire staff comes together as a whole group to list the themes, patterns, beliefs, and values that

Figure 2.1 Sample Distribution of Staff Members

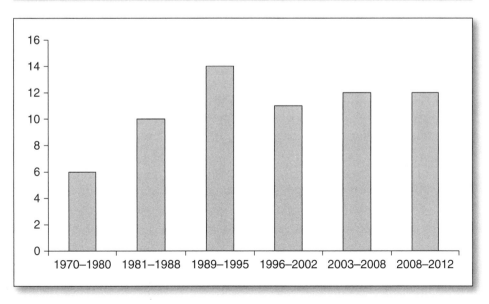

signified what worked. These aspects of the school's history become part of the vision for the school's future. This is an important capstone in the Historygram process. One of the elementary schools we worked with had a group that called themselves "Storytellers." They shared a tradition that began during their era that continues to this day. Each fall, student storytellers in each grade level write about their experiences from the previous year and then visit classrooms to tell their stories to the younger students. This tradition has continued at the school for over a decade, and teachers felt it was something worth keeping. Honoring what has worked in the past helps teachers to step into the unknown future with assurances that they are bringing with them pieces of what's worked and is familiar. No blank slates.

Developing Core Beliefs and Commitments

When was the last time you and your staff members developed a set of core beliefs that represent who you are and what you value as a professional community? Can you name the core beliefs of your organization? Identifying core beliefs and developing commitments to action that support those beliefs is an essential step in the change process.

Belief statements reflect what a group or school community believes to be true about a particular topic or issue. They are important because they express our values and in turn how we choose to act. For example, if I believe that all students can learn and that the quality of teaching is the most important factor impacting student learning, then as a teacher, I will seek out strategies and resources that facilitate learning for all. If, on the other hand, I believe that extrinsic factors, such as family environment or socioeconomic status play the greatest role in a child's ability to learn, I may rely on those factors to explain why that child is failing. Whether they relate to the capacity of students to learn, teacher responsibility for learning, the importance of collaboration and teacher learning, or the link between teaching and learning, belief statements provide powerful testaments that govern behavior and responses. These statements "or informal rules become 'organizational blueprints' that people are obliged to follow" (Deal & Petersen, 2009, p. 67). They are critical to the long term success of any change initiative, because they address the question teachers will ultimately ask, *why are we doing this*?

Let's take a look at a way to engage a group in developing statements that reflect their beliefs and aligned commitments. The example here is taken from the work I've done for over a decade with schools in helping them redesign their teacher evaluation systems. It would be an understatement to say this work is high stakes, bringing with it strong emotions that require many instances of risk taking and leaps of faith. It is change that begins with establishing a purpose. Why are we making this change? What purpose should teacher evaluation serve? What are our beliefs about teacher evaluation? What are we willing to commit to do in order to ensure that the new system is designed in service of this purpose?

The answers to these questions reveal the group's thinking and beliefs about teacher evaluation. The process of developing belief statements starts with a series of questions intended to help the group think about their views, experiences, and desired outcomes of the initiative. Prior to beginning any work on development of the new process and forms, members of the group are asked to consider what their role will be in the change process and how they will contribute to the work ahead. A sample list of questions is shown in Figure 2.2, Teacher Evaluation Design: Getting Started.

After the members of the group have had an opportunity to think and reflect on the topic, they are presented with research on best practices in teacher evaluation, such as the report by the New Teacher Project, *Teacher Evaluation 2.0* (2010) and *The Widget Effect* (Weisberg, Sexton, Mulhern, & Keeling, 2009). Group members read and then share important points from the research with their colleagues. Review of current research is an important step in developing belief statements because the system itself must be guided by best practices.

Next, the group members are asked to develop belief statements. Using sticky notes, each person takes a few moments to respond to the following statement:

This School District believes that the Teacher Evaluation Process must support . . .

Recording one idea on each sticky note, each person may write three to five ideas about their beliefs. After about five minutes, the group facilitator asks each person to share one idea with the group, telling why they believe it is important.

The next step is for the group to synthesize their thinking on chart paper. Using their sticky notes, they begin to cluster like ideas on the chart, giving each cluster a label. Each label is then written as a belief statement. A sample of Belief Statements and Commitments from Webster Central Schools in Webster, New York is shown in Figure 2.3.

Once the group has developed a set of belief statements, they must consider what actions will support these beliefs. Commitment statements are written in response to the following:

In order to embed these Teacher Evaluation Process beliefs into ongoing professional practice, this School District commits to . . .

Commitments should be written as action statements, representing *what you will do* to support these beliefs. Commitments are written for each belief statement.

These beliefs and commitments will guide the work of the group members as they make decisions about what they will keep doing, stop doing, and start doing in the new system. They reflect the core values and underlying assumptions about the topic and shape the future decisions and actions of the group and staff as a whole. These statements are posted at each subsequent meeting and referenced throughout the change process. Taking the time to develop beliefs and commitment statements is an important step in creating a culture for learning.

Demonstrating Beliefs: Actions of the School Leader

How do successful school leaders demonstrate their beliefs about teaching and learning? How are the core beliefs of the school community reflected in the actions of school leaders? If it's true that actions speak louder than words, what do school leaders *do* to demonstrate these beliefs?

As important as it is for schools to define their beliefs and commitments, it is equally important for school leaders to demonstrate these beliefs through their actions. Tom Sergiovanni describes the responsibility of school leaders to turn beliefs into actions in his essay, "The Virtues of School Leadership": "The heartbeats of leadership and schools are strengthened when word and deed are one" (2005, p. 112). School leaders develop an environment that fosters deep learning, problem solving and higher thinking skills based on their actions rather than words. What actions can school leaders take to create an environment where beliefs are demonstrated through actions each and every day?

Developing Trust and Rapport

As we established earlier in this chapter, changes in behavior usually precede changes in beliefs. Successful school leaders understand

Figure 2.2   Teacher Evaluation System Design: Getting Started

The following questions will help the group members think about the current evaluation process, the purpose and desired outcomes of this work, and the contributions each person will bring to this process. Be ready to share your thoughts!

1. What are some of the best attributes of the present evaluation system that should continue? ("Keep Doing")

2. What aspects of the present system could be improved, adjusted in some way, or added? ("Stop/Start Doing")

3. What expertise, insights, and effort are you committing to this process in order to make the experience and the end products successful?

4. When you think about the kinds of feedback you have received about your performance, or that you have given to another educator, what makes that kind of information useful or not useful? What must be included in the evaluation system that will trigger continuous growth?

5. What are some of the reasons for making changes in the teacher evaluation process, and what are some messages that staff will need to know about those reasons?

the importance of developing trust and rapport with staff as a prerequisite to changing behavior. As teachers are asked to change their instructional practice and try something new, they need to know that they will be supported by their leaders and that mistakes they make along the way will be seen as steps in the learning process.

Bryk and Schneider (2003) examined the conditions that foster trust in schools. The actions of the school principal, they found, were among the key factors in developing trust:

> Principals establish both respect and personal regard when they acknowledge the vulnerabilities of others, actively listen to their concerns, and eschew arbitrary actions. Effective principals couple these behaviors with a compelling school vision and behavior that clearly seeks to advance the vision. This consistency between words and actions affirms their personal integrity. (p. 43–44)

Teachers are the first to recognize the difference between school leaders who merely talk the talk, and those who walk the walk through their actions and deeds. One way that leaders demonstrate support for staff members is by encouraging them to develop their own leadership qualities and skills. Leaders send a strong message to teachers when they invite them to lead the learning with colleagues.

Figure 2.3 Teacher Evaluation

Belief/Commitment Statements	
Beliefs	**Aligned Commitments**
The Webster Central School district believes that teacher evaluation procedures must support improved student learning through:	**In order to embed these Teacher Evaluation Process beliefs into ongoing professional practice, this School District commits to:**
A Collaborative Culture based on trust, transparency and respect	• Open dialogue focused on instruction • Opportunities for sharing and celebration of strengths • Opportunities for professional collaboration within & outside of WCSD • Continuous growth within Professional Learning Communities
Research-based instructional practices supported by continuous professional growth and learning	• Utilizing the Framework for Teaching and accompanying rubrics as the agreed upon definition of effective teaching • Providing differentiated opportunities and resources to engage teachers in professional learning
Transparent procedures that are clear, consistent, reliable and evidence based	• Provide teachers with electronic access to the procedures & tools for evaluation • Using multiple measures in determining teach effectiveness • Respectful collaborative processes that allow for an evidence-based appraisal of teacher performance
Reflective practices	• Opportunities for collegial conversations that review evidence/artifacts of teaching and student learning • Embedding reflective practices in professional learning experiences

Rather than leading the learning as a sage on the stage, successful leaders step aside and lead by participating in learning alongside the teachers as a guide on the side.

Step Aside and Lead: Creating Opportunities for Learning

Leaders who believe in the capacity of their staff demonstrate this belief by creating opportunities for teachers to seek help from one another; share materials, resources, and strategies; experiment with new approaches to teaching content or skills; and contribute to decisions that impact their daily work. Common planning time, faculty meetings, department or grade level meetings, and conference days are regarded as protected opportunities for teacher learning. School leaders who understand how teacher learning occurs and believe in their need for autonomy provide teachers the opportunity to lead and participate in activities that are meaningful and relevant.

More importantly, they recognize the need to make public the contributions and to share the success stories of teachers. As Robert Evans (1996) wrote in his book, *The Human Side of Change,* "The single-best, low-cost, high-leverage way to improve performance, morale and the climate for change is to dramatically increase the levels of meaningful recognition for—and among—educators." He went on to say that we have sorely neglected the need for adults to be recognized and celebrated for their accomplishments and that we "shower recognition on pupils but deny it to adults" (p. 254–256).

Leaders who walk the walk of their beliefs about teaching and learning are those we mentioned earlier who can most often be found in the classroom, observing, listening, and learning. They don't wait for a spare moment to present itself to follow up with the teacher whose classroom they've visited. They intentionally seek out the teacher and engage them in conversation, reflection and professional dialogue. These conversations may only last a few minutes, but they send a powerful message to teachers about the leader's role in supporting quality instruction.

Leaders who demonstrate their beliefs through actions attend professional development alongside their teachers. They don't watch from the sidelines; they join a group of teachers and participate as a learner. They demonstrate the importance of continuous learning by choosing to participate in learning rather than using the time to finish up administrative tasks. They willingly participate in challenging learning because they are driven by a growth mindset that sees challenge as an opportunity to grow rather than fail.

Key Points About Creating a Culture of Learning

School leaders today are faced with challenging the status quo. The Lake Wobegon effect has created a culture of nice where all teaching is rated above average. As a result, improving teacher quality has not been viewed as a priority in many schools.

The current landscape, however, is changing, with new demands on teachers and school leaders to evaluate the quality of teaching based on multiple measures, including measures of student learning. One of the results of looking at teacher quality through this new lens will be increased levels of feedback and criticism around instructional practice. Successful school leaders will be able to help teachers change existing mindsets that fear constructive criticism and feedback and create school environments where continuous learning for all is a cultural norm.

School leaders who are successful in creating a culture of learning are propelled by certain dispositions and beliefs about teaching and learning. They demonstrate their beliefs by honoring the school's history and developing core beliefs about teaching and learning that drive commitments to action. Leaders who believe that improving the quality of teaching is their most important responsibility make choices that demonstrate this belief. They regularly visit classrooms, engage in collegial conversations, and provide teachers with opportunities to grow and learn from each other. They lead with a growth mindset, acknowledging the risks and challenges inherent in learning but more importantly, acknowledging its rewards. They are not threatened by impending changes to the school landscape because they believe in the capacity of the teachers to grow and learn. A school leader who demonstrates these beliefs through action creates a culture of learning for all—leaders, teachers, and, ultimately, for students.

What do school leaders need to know about staff, about effective practice, about learning, in order to make the most of a culture of learning? In the next chapter, we'll examine the understandings and skills that that are central to instructional leadership and improving the quality of teaching.

Putting Words Into Action

Reflecting on Your Current State

• Can you recall a time when an experience you had changed your beliefs about teaching or learning? It may have been a conversation you had with a teacher or student, a project you organized or participated in, a course you took (possibly alongside the teachers), a class you taught, a new resource you discovered, or even a place you visited. How might this experience be used in your role as a leader to help others understand that practice drives beliefs?

- What are the core beliefs of your organization? How are they communicated to staff members? When was the last time they were reviewed? Can you think of an example when you referred to the core beliefs in a conversation with staff?

Action Tools

- Capture the History
  - o Use the process described in Figure 2.4 to capture your school's traditions and history.

- Promote Professional Reading.
  - o One of the ways to encourage professional learning is to provide access to current research and articles that are available online. Invite staff to engage in professional reading by sending a copy or a link to the Table of Contents page from one or two educational journals to teachers and professional staff members each month such as the *American Educational Research Journal, Journal of Staff Development,* or *Educational Leadership.* You may even include a recommendation of an article you've read to spur interest and awareness of a relevant topic.

Figure 2.4   A Process for Capturing School History

Where, When, and Why
   Schedule a time and place for the faculty to participate in this activity. It is important to communicate the purpose of this meeting to all participants. The meeting will be an opportunity for staff members to come together to reflect and understand the patterns, cycles, and trends of the collective organizational history of the school. The purpose is to understand where the organization has been in the past and to create a shared vision for the future.
The Process:

   1.   Before the meeting begins, tape a long piece of paper to one wall (or possibly around the room) and draw a time line from one end of the paper to the other, ending with an arrow and a cloud marked "Future". Do not label the timeline until the meeting starts.

   2.   As the meeting begins, explain that telling stories about the past is a way to help schools understand where they have been and to understand where they are going in the future. Acknowledge that there are many events in the school history that teachers who were hired in recent years may be unaware of. This process will capture those events, creating a historical memory of the organization's culture.

3.   Ask who has been with the organization the longest and when that person was hired. Record the year he or she started at the beginning of the time line and invite the person to stand in front of that "era" on the time line. You may also invite this tribal elder to tell a short anecdote about what the school was like back then.

4.   Invite the rest of the staff to form a line along the wall in the order of when they were first hired by the district, starting from earliest to most recent. If a number of people joined the organization in the same year, have them stand one behind another, with the most senior person at the front of the line. For years when no one was hired (an interesting part of organizational history in itself), make spaces between the lines. In this way, a human histogram forms. As members line up, the years are recorded on the chart.

5.   After everyone has lined up, group the years into eras which are usually based on a five to ten year span, depending on the number of people who occupy those years. The sample in Figure 2.1 has six eras.

6.   Members of each era receive chart paper and discuss the following questions:

  ○ What would be an appropriate name for this era? (For example, "The Birth of Technology")
  ○ What was the culture like? What tribal stories circulated? What symbols and ceremonies were important?
  ○ What were the major initiatives?
  ○ What were the goals of each initiative?
  ○ How was the success of the initiatives measured? How did you know that you were making progress? What was the basis for shifting direction?
  ○ What values from the past do you want to bring into the future?

The group decides on a name for the era and then captures the story about their era on chart paper.

7.   Volunteers from each group are invited to tell the rest of the group the story about that era. As the stories unfold, ask participants to identify patterns, trends, and cycles. Look for underlying assumptions that people are making about why people behaved as they did in the past, why changes were initiated, and what the goals were in each era. These questions inevitably lead to a rich conversation and a deep understanding about the organization's history, an important step in learning how mental models have been formed and how they have shaped actions.

8.   Once the process has been completed, ask the group to consider the following questions:

  ○ *Keep Doing:* What values and behaviors from the past will we take with us into the future?
  ○ *Start Doing:* What promises can we make to one another to better fulfill our purpose? What do we need to do as a group, team, or as individuals to move forward?
  ○ *Stop Doing:* What behaviors, beliefs, or assumptions can we leave in the past?

3

The Wisdom of Instructional Leadership

What Leaders Need to Know and Do

You can't lead what you don't know.

Dr. Valerie Henning-Piedmonte

Much has been written in the last two decades on the topic of instructional leadership, with the intent to guide principals and school leaders in how to teach the teachers. Outstanding principals, they say, know that their primary role is to teach teachers. Todd Whitaker states, "Great principals focus on students—by focusing on teachers" (2003, p. 35), and he argues that there are basically two ways to improve schools: hire better teachers or improve the teachers you have. A principal's ability to select the best teachers and to mentor and support them by providing opportunities for professional development is paramount to their role as instructional leader.

When Jim Collins (2001) studied companies that successfully made a transformation from good to great, he found the attributes of

Level 5 leadership, the type required for turning a good company into a great one, required a specific skill when selecting and hiring staff:

> We expected that good-to-great leaders would begin by setting a new vision and strategy. We found instead that they *first* got the right people on the bus, the wrong people off the bus, and the right people in the right seats—and *then* figured out where to drive it. The old adage "People are your most important asset" turns out to be wrong. People are *not* your most important asset. The *right* people are. (p.13)

Who are the *right* people? How do you know if you've got the *wrong* people on the bus? What can a school leader do to improve the teachers he has? Selecting the right teachers and helping them to become the best teachers requires specific knowledge, skills, and understandings on the part of the school leader. The premise of this chapter is that leaders cannot lead what they do not know. If they do not have certain knowledge, understandings, and skills about teaching and learning, they cannot improve the quality of teaching in their schools. Current literature available on the topic of instructional leadership lists the elements of effective instructional leaders. Topics covered include visioning, developing the school culture, shared leadership, teacher evaluation, data analysis, monitoring curriculum and instruction, operations and building management, and more. But how does one evaluate the quality of teaching without understanding the components of effective practice? How can a school leader who doesn't know the difference between student compliance and student engagement monitor instruction? I believe that much of the available literature for school leaders is written with the assumption that leaders *know* what good teaching is and how learning occurs. It directs leaders to "look for the teachers who will be exceptional in the classroom" to "hire teachers who have a love of students, a bright mind, a positive attitude, a congenial personality . . . " *What does this mean?*

This chapter examines the wisdom of successful leaders, specifically what leaders need to know about their staff, about teaching and learning, and what skills they will need in order to hire, grow, and improve the quality of teachers under their leadership.

Knowledge of Staff

One of the questions I pose to teachers when meeting them for the first time is, "What do you believe are the attributes of exemplary teachers? If you were to envision the teacher you would aspire to be someday, how would you describe him or her?" I've asked this question hundreds of times in schools of every size, location, and demographic—from veteran teachers to first year newbies. The most common answer to this question relates to their knowledge of students as learners, and their ability to connect with students on a level that allows learning to occur. Teachers recognize the importance of knowing their students in making learning both rigorous and meaningful. They know that learners don't come in one size, that they all bring strengths in different areas, and that each student begins learning at a different starting point. Great teachers select learning outcomes, materials and resources, activities, and assignments based on the needs of the learners. They communicate based on the student's learning style, confidence level, and their relationship with the student. They know which students work best with others, and those who learn best on their own. They know their students well enough to be able to determine how challenging a task needs to be in order for it to be rigorous *for that student.*

We can apply this same line of thinking to the relationship between school leaders and teachers. Successful instructional leadership begins with knowing your students—the teachers and professionals who comprise your staff. Improving the quality of teaching involves learning—teacher learning. When we consider what leaders need to know, we can apply everything we know about student learning to this conversation.

Let's return to our friend Gary, the principal of Washington Elementary School who we met in Chapter One. Most would agree that Gary successfully created a culture of nice in his building. He maintained a positive rapport with teachers, many of whom would tell you that they liked working under Gary's leadership, and that, although they felt pressure from impending changes to their jobs from the state and national level, they felt supported and safe in their positions. If we were to ask Gary to describe his staff, we would recognize from his responses that he knew them as people: how many children they had, favorite hobbies or sports they participated in, favorite team, if they were a morning person (always to school early) or a "last minute" person (last to arrive at meetings or handing in paperwork), an extrovert or introvert, and so on. He definitely had a good sense of his teachers personally. But what about who they were professionally? What was their developmental level around pedagogy and practice? What was their learning style? Were they self-directed, preferring to learn on their own, or did they learn best when supported by others and collaborating with peers? Did they approach teaching and learning with a growth mindset or fixed?

A leader who doesn't know his teachers as professionals is at an extreme disadvantage—for a number of reasons. First, let's acknowledge the fact the teachers in any school are that school's greatest resource. Collectively, they bring a wealth of experience, skills, understanding, and potential for improving opportunities for students. In addition, most teachers remain in their positions far longer than their supervisors. Walk into any school today and ask veteran teachers how many principals they've had since they started working in the district. It's likely that they have outlasted their administrators several times over. Research conducted on the tenure and retention of principals found that more than one out of every five principals leaves their school each year (Beteille, Kalogrides, & Loeb, 2011). A study of newly hired high school principals in Texas found that just over 50 percent stay for three years and less than 30 percent stay for five years (Fuller & Young, 2009).

If we recognize that teachers are the most valuable asset to a school, then we need leaders who are able to tap into their collective talent and potential for improving schools. This is impossible unless we know our teachers as professionals and understand the potential contributions each teacher can make to improving teaching and learning. Leaders who don't know their staff as professionals are missing out on a valuable (and inexpensive) resource for improving schools.

With all of the recent focus on teacher retention and attrition, it was interesting to come across an article titled, "Why Great Teachers Stay" (Williams, 2003) in my research. The purpose of the article was to examine why teachers choose to remain in a profession where others are opting out or burning out. Twelve teachers who had been in the classroom an average of twenty-three years were interviewed about the characteristics of the workplace that made their jobs professionally fulfilling and contributed to their success in the classroom. Without exception, teachers mentioned the need for intellectual stimulation, opportunities for creativity, and variation as prime motivators in their work. "Change energizes and refreshes them; they are willing to take risks" (Williams, 2003, p. 71). These exemplary teachers credited their administrators for "setting the right mix of challenge and support that enables schools to become joyful, productive places" (Williams, 2003, p. 74).

Great teachers stick around when they are provided with an opportunity to learn and grow, in areas that are meaningful and relevant, and in ways that fit their learning style and developmental level. School leaders can't possibly offer these opportunities to teachers unless they know the teachers as learners. Similar to the knowledge we expect teachers to have of their students, school leaders must know their staff.

How do leaders get to know their staff? By spending time where teachers spend *their* time—in classrooms, department meetings, workshops, seminars, conferences, collegial circles, or study groups. By engaging with teachers in professional conversations that dig deeply into instructional practice and learning. By creating opportunities for teachers to share and showcase their success in engaging students in learning. By creating a culture where you don't have to be bad to get better—we are all learners. Finally, leaders get to know their staff by believing in their competence and potential to grow and learn, and by providing opportunities for them to do so.

Understandings About Teaching and Learning

To improve the quality of teaching, one must first have an understanding what quality teaching *is.* "I know good teaching when I see it" simply won't work. Leaders have long been criticized for their lack of consistency when defining effective practice. Similarly, leaders need to be on the same page in answering the question, "How good is good enough?" They need to understand the attributes of effective practice and the indicators of each level of performance.

To engage teachers in learning, school leaders need to understand the nature of learning and how it occurs. When observing instruction, leaders need to be able to distinguish between a compliant classroom and one where students are engaged in learning.

What Is Good Teaching?

It is difficult, if not impossible, for anyone to talk about how to improve the quality of teaching without first establishing a common language about effective practice. Many schools want to immediately jump to the *how* without first understanding the *what*. Under pressure from state and local authorities to meet deadlines, in jeopardy of losing funding if they don't submit a plan for the "process" by the due date, schools are rushing right past the first step: understanding the components of effective practice.

One of the most recognized and widely used publications in the field of teacher learning and teacher evaluation is Charlotte Danielson's *Enhancing Professional Practice: A Framework for Teaching* (2007). The

Framework offers a research-based, comprehensive definition of teaching structured around four domains: planning and preparation, classroom environment, instruction, and professional responsibilities. It recognizes the relationships between what occurs in the classroom and what happens beyond the classroom. It provides educators with what Danielson calls a "road map" structured around the territory of the complex work of teaching.

Without a set of teaching standards to guide their work, instructional leaders are left playing guessing games when engaging in the duties of instructional leadership. When visiting a classroom, what should I be looking for? What's most important? What if I don't see something *I know* is important? When speaking with a new teacher who is struggling with managing student behavior, how can I help the teacher make the connection between classroom behavior and instructional planning? When teachers meet with me for a pre-observation conference, what should we be talking about? Are there specific components of planning that lead to success in the classroom?

An experience I had years ago when I was supervising preservice teachers for a small college in Rochester, New York provides a powerful example of how leaders can apply their understanding of teaching standards to promote teacher learning. I call it the story of the sword fight, appropriately named as you will read.

Karen was a thirty-five-year-old professional who was entering the teaching profession as a second career. When I arrived for a scheduled observation, she was about three weeks into her student teaching placement in a fifth-grade classroom in Seneca Falls, New York. She had sent me a copy of her lesson plan in advance, a mini-lesson that would begin the language arts block. The student learning outcome was learning to take notes from expository text. Karen was beginning a unit on famous women and had chosen a piece of text she found about the life of Susan B. Anthony. The Women's Rights National Hall of Fame is located in Seneca Falls, making both the topic as well as the subject matter very relevant to students.

To begin the lesson, students were seated in groups of four or five, and Karen was at the front of the room with a copy of the text projected onto a large screen. Each student was provided with a copy of the same text, and a yellow highlighter. Karen began by introducing the learning objective to students, taking notes from expository text. After reviewing the term "expository" by soliciting examples from the students, she directed them to read along with her as she read the first two paragraphs of text aloud. As she read, she highlighted several statements then turned to a chart pad where she recorded the highlights in bulleted form. As she read the text aloud, I wondered about the level of difficulty of the reading. Having taught fifth grade for several years, I was concerned that it might be too much of a stretch for most students. Being a visitor in the classroom, I reserved my initial judgment and continued to look and listen.

After Karen had modeled the process with the whole group, she directed the students to continue reading the remainder of the hand-out, highlighting important points and capturing them in a bulleted group list. She told the reporters in each group they needed to be ready to share their list with the rest of the class in ten minutes. "Any questions? Ok, get started."

During the next sixty seconds, the learning environment became one of chaos, confusion, and clamor. Confused, agitated students who were unable to comprehend what they were reading responded by raising their hands, calling out to the teacher for help, crumpling up their paper in frustration, or simply giving up. Except for one group, seated directly in front of me (of course). They decided that a better use of their highlighters would be to stick them together, end to end, and have a sword fight. Very clever use of materials, but not exactly what Karen had intended!

Needless to say, when Karen and I sat down to debrief the lesson, she was visibly upset. "I should never have left my job at Xerox. I can't manage a classroom of twenty-six children! It's too hard. I know that students need to work in groups, but every time I try this arrangement, all hell breaks loose! Can you help me with this? Do you have any suggestions for managing student behavior? I'll try anything!"

Was managing student behavior the issue we needed to discuss? Did the chaos result because Karen was unable to control behavior in the classroom? Student behavior certainly *became* a problem, but it was not the *cause* of the problem. Using the teaching standards of the *Framework for Teaching* as a guide, our conversation headed in an entirely different direction. I asked Karen to consider the four domains of professional practice and think about what caused students to become frustrated and to give up. She was quick to identify that the text was too difficult for students to read, something she had not considered in planning. New to teaching fifth grade, she was unfamiliar with their reading levels and chose an easily accessed resource about Susan B. Anthony to use for the mini-lesson. She admitted that there were likely many more appropriate resources available to use in a lesson with fifth graders, especially in Seneca Falls! Karen learned a valuable lesson about the relationship between student engagement, knowledge of students, and knowledge of resources. Knowing the teaching standards, I was able to steer Karen's thinking to the cause of her lesson's downfall. Rather than spend our time troubleshooting student behavior or trying to guess what went wrong, we were able to have a productive conversation about the importance of planning and choosing materials and resources.

Another important reason why school leaders need to know and understand the components of effective teaching relates to consistency in observing practice. Ask any group of teachers what causes their greatest frustration when visited by administrators—most surely they will mention a lack of consistency. When leaders haven't developed a common understanding of the components of effective teaching, inconsistencies and bias emerge. Instead of using a common set of standards to guide, observe, discuss, and support effective teaching, leaders end up putting their own spin on these expectations. Teachers are the first to recognize a lack of agreement among school leaders on what effective teaching *really is.* Although they can never be entirely eliminated, school leaders can take steps to reduce inconsistencies by adopting and learning a common language that defines effective practice.

How Good Is Good Enough?

How can school leaders use a set of teaching standards, such as the Framework, to promote reliability and consistency in observing and evaluating the quality of teaching? What prevents the accepted set of teaching standards from simply becoming a checklist for school leaders?

We don't have to look far to find a school system that provides "feedback" to teachers (and I use that term very lightly) about the quality of their work using one (or more) of the following labels:

- Unsatisfactory, Satisfactory, or Not Applicable
- Observed or Not Observed
- Needs Improvement, Acceptable, or Highly Acceptable
- 1, 2, 3, or 4
- Unsatisfactory, Improvement Needed, or Meets Professional Standards

What, exactly, does a "3" mean? What is the difference between "Needs Improvement" and "Unsatisfactory"? "Highly Acceptable" and "Acceptable"? Is a "4" at the middle school the same as a "4" at the high school? These labels do nothing to improve the quality of teaching because they are neither reliable nor descriptive. They fail to provide critical information about the quality of teaching to either the teacher or the school leader.

To improve the quality of teaching, both leaders and teachers need to understand what these labels mean and develop indicators and possible examples for each level. This requires training, practice, and conversation among both leaders and teachers. As these understandings are developed, teachers and leaders can use the levels of performance for reflecting on practice, setting goals for improvement, developing new strategies for teaching and learning, and engaging in collegial dialogue that results in teacher learning. Far too often, standards of performance adopted by states and local school districts are seen and used for nothing other than teacher evaluation, offering a summative score and rank for teachers. Clearly defined standards of performance that answer the question, "How good is good enough?" provide a valuable tool for school leaders to offer formative feedback that improves the quality of teaching.

How Does Learning Occur?

What do leaders need to know about learning? Lee Shulman writes about "Teachers as Learners" in his book, *The Wisdom of Practice* (2004). He confirms our earlier statement about the relationship between teacher learning and student learning, "I believe the conditions for teacher learning are directly parallel to those needed for pupil learning" (Shulman, 2004, p. 513). Two of the most important principles that cause teacher learning he writes, are activity and reflection. Teachers who are active in talking with one another, sharing information, and challenging one another's ideas are learning. They learn through activities requiring mental work such as experimentation and inquiry, writing, dialogue, and questioning. They are "active investigators of their own teaching" (Shulman, 2004, p. 514).

Learning does not occur, however, with mere activity. As John Dewey recognized many years ago, we do not learn just by doing; we learn by thinking about what we are doing. Reflection is a key component of learning. Teachers need to be provided with opportunities to reflect, self-assess, and apply their reflections to future actions. Some teachers prefer journaling in private to record and analyze their thinking; others reflect in collaboration and conversation with colleagues, during study groups or collegial circles, or even in less formal settings after school. For some teachers, collaboration offers the opportunity to wrestle with difficult intellectual and cognitive challenges that may be impossible to resolve alone.

The essential understanding that leaders need about learning can be captured in a phrase coined by my colleague, Charlotte Danielson, "Learning is done by the learner." How simple, yet how often overlooked. Danielson (2009) writes, "We tend to think our students learn because of what *we* do. . . . Our students don't learn because of what *we* do, they learn because of what *they* do" (p. 36). The impact for school leaders is profound. Rather than delivering professional development into the laps of teachers through a "sit and get" presentation that requires no mental activity on their part, leaders must respect the nature of learning and put learning in the hands of the learner. They must step aside and allow the teachers to step up. Only then will teachers grow and improve the quality of their teaching.

What Is Engagement in Learning?

> You don't just learn knowledge; you have to
> create it. Get in the driver's seat, don't just be
> a passenger. You have to contribute to it or you
> don't understand it.
>
> Dr. W. Edwards Deming

Whenever I speak with a group of educators on the topic of learning and what causes learning to occur, this quote from Dr. Deming is always a favorite of mine to use. As a matter of fact, this "car" metaphor has become the lens that I use when observing classrooms in search of student engagement. We'll take a closer look at the car metaphor later on.

Engaging students in learning is the *sine qua non* of teaching. Everything teachers do is in the service of student engagement. As such, it is critical that school leaders understand what it means and how to recognize engagement (or the lack of it) in the classroom. As we've already mentioned, you can't lead what you don't know.

When I design learning experiences for school leaders for the purpose of building their capacity as instructional leaders, there are many topics from which to choose. Developing their understanding of student engagement is at the top of my list. If teaching is the most important, school-based factor that impacts student learning and engaging students in learning is the primary responsibility of teaching, how can school leaders play a role in improving the quality of teaching without a solid understanding of student engagement?

At this point, you may be saying to yourself, "Of course principals know what student engagement is. That's taught in Education 101! Anyone who's ever taught knows this." Well, not exactly. At the start of our training, we take a "before" snapshot by asking participants to jot down the words or phrases that come to mind when they think about student engagement. I ask them to imagine they are responding to a friend who has an upcoming interview for a teaching position with the school district, and they need to know what to say about student engagement. Later on, when we've completed the learning activity, they will revisit these words and reflect on how their understanding has changed. As they go around the room, sharing their initial ideas, I hear words like: time on task, hands-on, working in groups, using manipulatives, and active participation. Although there are similarities in the words used to describe engagement, there is no consensus regarding its definition or what might constitute evidence of engagement. Lacking a clear, common understanding of student engagement, school leaders are left to rely on their own interpretations.

A study published in the journal *Psychology in Schools* (Appleton, Christenson, & Furlong, 2008) found the same inconsistencies in the way student engagement was defined and conceptualized. Researchers cited numerous variations in the definitions and interpretations of student engagement. They explained a lack of clarity in defining the construct engagement:

> The short, approximately 22-year history of engagement highlights its need for a clear definition. Although uses of this construct have proliferated, definitional clarity has been elusive. The theoretical and research literatures on engagement generally reflect little consensus about definitions and contain substantial variations in how engagement is operationalized and measured. (Appleton, Christenson, & Furlong, 2008, p. 369)

Fortunately, there is ample research on cognition and learning, which is where our definition of student engagement originates:

- There is a clear consensus among researchers that all students, perhaps at-risk students especially, require instruction that is cognitively challenging; that is, that requires thinking and analysis, not only rote, repetitive, detail-level drills (Tharp, Estrada, Dalton, &Yamauchi, 2000, p. 30–31).

- What is required for student engagement is *intellectual involvement* with the content or active construction of understanding. . . . What is required is *mental engagement*, which may or may not involve physical activity. Hands-on is not enough, it must be "minds on" (Danielson, 2007, p. 83).

- Thought is how we learn. . . . students think *as* they learn, not *after* they learn. (Strong, Silver, & Perini, 2001, p. 34–5).

- Learning means constructing, creating, inventing, and developing your own knowledge. It is the process and the result of questioning, interpreting, and analyzing information (Marlowe & Page, 2005, p. 7.)

- Engagement relates to the extent to which students are actively involved in their own learning. Learning experiences at the low end of engagement require little thinking or doing on the part of students . . . highly engaging activities require intentionality, focus, and energy, both physical and mental, on the part of students (Martin-Kniep & Picone-Zocchia, 2009, p. 13).

- "Learning without thought is labor lost; and thought without learning is perilous" (Confucius).

Student engagement requires cognition; it is mental work. Learning is the result of decisions teachers make in designing instruction to create opportunities that require students to think. This means thinking by all students, simultaneously and continuously, throughout the lesson. A classroom where three or four students are doing all of the mental work engages three or four students in learning. Students must be challenged to think at a level that is cognitively demanding and rigorous. When all students are required to complete the same task or assignment, the level of challenge will be appropriate for some, but not all. Student engagement requires pushing students to extend their thinking and to reach beyond their current capacities, to spend emotional, intellectual, and sometimes physical energy. Learning is work, mental work.

When you think about something you've learned really well, a concept you deeply understand, a topic you know well, a skill you can perform with precision, or a demonstration you have perfected – how did you learn? What did you do? Let's return to the car metaphor. Most adults have a license to drive a car. How did that learning occur? By reading a book about driving? Watching NASCAR? By riding in a car? None of the above. We learn how to drive by driving the car. We learned by doing the mental and physical work involved in driving a car. We made decisions about when to turn on the blinker in advance of a turn, how much room we needed to come to a complete stop, whether or not there was room to pass the car ahead of us, and so on. As we said earlier, learning is done by the learner. It's a thinking person's job requiring mental work.

When I enter a classroom, the question I ask myself is, "Who is doing the mental work?" I think about the students in terms of where they are seated in the car. Are they *in* the car? Or, as in some unfortunate cases, are they standing on the side of the road as the car whizzes by? Are students sitting in the back seat, the front seat, or are they in the driver's seat, leading the learning? Are all of the students in the same place, or has the learning been differentiated to accommodate the needs of all students in the class? How do I know? What are the signs of student engagement?

Student engagement takes many forms. How engagement is evidenced depends on a number of factors, such as the learning outcome, the content and skills being taught, the students in the classroom, the physical arrangement of the room, and how students are grouped, as well as the materials and resources that are used during the lesson. In a physical education class, evidence of engagement may involve a new skill or strategy used to defend an opponent; in a music class it may be evident in the adjustments students make to their performance based on feedback from the teacher; in an elementary math class it may be evidenced by the discoveries students share with one another about the volume and capacity of containers they've filled; in a language arts class it may be evident in the responses students write in their journals about what they've read.

Leaders, armed with an understanding of student engagement, are now ready to pose the question to teachers, "What are the signs of student engagement that *you* look for during a lesson? That is what *I* will look for." Although school leaders need to understand the concept of engagement in learning, it is ultimately the responsibility of the classroom teacher to know what it looks like in his classroom. Armed with this understanding, leaders are able to support teachers by providing them with the resources needed to increase the level of student engagement and learning in the classroom.

Skills of the Instructional Leader

Gaining an understanding about standards for professional practice, the nature of learning, and student engagement is a prerequisite for improving the quality of teaching. Without this knowledge, leaders are not able to reliably assess and develop the quality of teaching that currently exists among their staff members. To improve the quality of teaching, school leaders *apply their understanding* of teaching and learning using skills that enable them to assess teaching performance, communicate with teachers through professional conversation, and facilitate the development of professional goals for teacher learning. To have any chance of improving practice in their schools, these essential skills must be learned and practiced.

Collecting Evidence to Assess Teaching

Helping teachers grow and improve their practice begins by knowing their strengths and areas for growth. As mentioned earlier, learners don't come in one size. They have different needs and learning styles; they possess different skills and understandings. One of the aims of understanding the components of effective practice is to be able to assess teaching proficiency and develop a plan for growth and improvement.

The two main opportunities leaders have to collect evidence and assess teaching are observing classroom practice and engaging in professional conversations with teachers. They apply their understanding of the teaching standards and know what to look for when entering a classroom. They are able to recognize student engagement (or a lack thereof) when they see it. They know if a teacher has met the mark in any of the standards of teaching because those marks have been clearly established and communicated.

One of the most important rules in assessing the quality of teaching is that *evidence anchors the process*. It is dangerous to make decisions that impact teacher retention, tenure, or, in some cases, pay, in the absence of evidence to support the assessment. And yet, I've read hundreds of reports prepared by school leaders from coast to coast in districts large and small, urban, suburban, and rural, awarding honors and accolades or criticism and condemnation, without any comments that can be remotely construed as evidence to back them up. I can think of no other profession where we hand down judgments in the lack of evidence as cavalierly as we do in education. A court of law requires that evidence be produced to make a judgment about the guilt or innocence of a defendant charged with a crime. A doctor requires evidence to make a diagnosis. A coach requires evidence to replace his starting quarterback with the backup. A conductor requires evidence to choose his first violinist to lead the orchestra. Evidence is the anchor. Recognizing what constitutes evidence of teaching and developing the skills to collect evidence is an essential tool for school leaders.

Simply stated, evidence is "just the facts." It may include *specific* statements, actions, behaviors, materials, or artifacts that are seen and heard—from the teacher, students, parents, or colleagues. *Specific* is a key word here. I always direct observers in training to look at the statements they are writing to document an observation, conversation, or analysis of an artifact. If there are any words or phrases in the statement that can be interpreted in more than one way, then it isn't specific and is not evidence. For example, if an observer writes, "The teacher asked high level questions." What does "high level" mean? Can it have more than one interpretation? Of course it can. How do we know that the questions are *high level* for the students in that classroom? Evidence would be a direct quote from the teacher along with the student's response to a specific question. For example, the teacher asked, "Tell your elbow partner which character you believe was the bravest and provide two examples from the text to support your choice." Another example that is frequently written in observer's notes is, "Students are engaged—," or "Students are on task." What does that mean? Can "on task" be interpreted more than one way? Evidence would state exactly what students were doing or saying that the observer may have interpreted as "on task." For example, "Students were examining the petri dishes and recording observations in their journals."

Why is it important to record the facts and not a summary or interpretation of the facts? Specific evidence provides leaders with the opportunity to provide specific feedback to teachers that is fair, reliable, and valid. It eliminates the chance for bias or personal preferences to color the judgment or the conversation. If a leader says to a teacher, "Your directions were confusing," the teacher may respond, "No they weren't." However, if the leader shares the following evidence, "When students began the group activity, students asked, 'Are we supposed to use our textbook?', 'Can we work with a partner?', 'How much time do we have?', 'Didn't we do this for homework?'" the evidence removes any personal criticism and allows the conversation to focus on helping the teacher provide clear directions and check for understanding before moving to group work.

Compliments and accolades are much more meaningful when they are specific and stated as evidence. When my daughter was in school, the comment, "Kendall is a pleasure to have in class" appeared frequently on progress reports. Although I knew she was a good student and a likely pleasure for most teachers to have in class, the comment would have been so much more meaningful if it described what, exactly, made her such a pleasure. For example, the teacher could have stated, "Whenever we have a substitute teacher, Kendall always helps the teacher find materials and supplies." Or, "When a student needs to borrow supplies, Kendall is always willing to share." These specific examples would have made the comment more authentic, personal, and meaningful to me, but more importantly, to Kendall. The same is true for the feedback we provide to teachers. Specific statements that capture evidence of the teacher's skill, contributions, growth, and professionalism provide powerful feedback.

Have you ever come across an observation report or teacher evaluation that had another teacher's name embedded in the narrative? Unfortunately, this happens all too often. In the absence of specific feedback and evidence, all of the reports begin to look the same. As a result, teachers will focus on the rating, rather than the feedback, because the feedback is nothing more than generic gobbledygook they've read time after time. Collecting and recording evidence is the only way to provide specific feedback that improves the quality of teaching. When teachers collect specific evidence of student learning, they are able to assess learning and provide specific, constructive feedback that promotes student growth. The same principle applies to teacher learning.

Collecting and recording evidence takes practice. For many, it requires a shift in thinking and approach. To make this new approach manageable for learners, it's best to begin by focusing on one or two standards of teaching, such as student engagement or managing the learning environment, and then practice, practice, practice. Frequent, short visits provide opportunities to collect evidence, engage in conversation with the teacher, and measure the quality of teaching using the agreed upon standards.

Engaging in Professional Conversations

Professional conversations that improve the quality of teaching require the use of specific skills. These skills are most effective when used in a culture of professional learning where there is a presumption of continuous learning for all, described in Chapter Two. The skill set presented in this chapter is grounded in the research and literature on coaching:

> Coaching conversations are an essential tool for the twenty-first century leader. Coaching is a way of listening and speaking to colleagues that assumes a belief that others are

whole and capable. Others don't need to be "fixed." (Cheliotes & Reilly, 2010, p. 9)

These conversations are highly intentional, with the goal of engaging teachers in thinking that results in growth and change in practice. Professional conversations are so important to teacher learning that we have devoted an entire chapter to this topic. Here, we examine the skill set needed to make professional conversations productive.

Skillful Questioning

The most important linguistic skill for administrators and supervisors lies in asking the right questions and asking them in the right manner (Danielson, 2009). This statement represents no small task. There are a number of factors that contribute to skillful questioning. A key factor lies in the culture, tone, and rapport that exist between the leader and teacher. Another factor that impacts the success of questioning is the leader's knowledge of instructional practice. In an interview published in the Harvard Education Letter (Walser, 2011), Thomas Fowler-Finn describes what it takes to become an instructional leader. "Instructional leaders," he writes, "are most effective when asking the tough questions about student learning, not when giving answers. They learn what questions to ask through on-site experiences, not in university classrooms"(Walser, 2011, p. 1). The underlying assumption of this statement is that leaders know what questions to ask because they understand the standards for effective teaching. This is a very important point. On-site visits provide plenty of raw data that leaders can use during a conversation. Choosing the right data to ask the right questions relies upon the leader's understanding of teaching and learning, which we established earlier in this chapter.

Skillful questions that engage teachers in doing the mental work

- Are asked with positive intentions and a presumption of competence, not criticism
- Are asked at the teacher's "just right" level, intended to push at the limits of the teacher's capacity
- Are open ended
- May have more than one correct response
- Serve to extend the teacher's thinking, going beyond typical and routine
- Help teachers think deeply and develop their own ideas

Sample questions that promote teacher thinking and reflection are shared in Figure 3.1.

Productive Listening

Listening is something we all do every day. It may or may not involve any thinking. We may use our sense of hearing without really thinking about what we've heard. Have you ever told a significant other in your life, "I know you hear me, you're just not listening!"? Productive listening requires a commitment by the listener to focus their attention and energy on the message communicated by verbal and nonverbal means. It requires the listener to set aside unproductive patterns of listening. Cheliotes and Reilly (2010) list four patterns to avoid. As you read, think about your own tendencies when listening. Do you identify with one or more of these unproductive patterns?

1. *Judgment or criticism*—Here, a negative judgment has already been made toward the speaker. The listener has already decided that nothing positive or worthwhile will be said by the speaker. Rather than listen with an open mind, looking for opportunities for growth, the listener shuts down the speaker's thinking, leading to a loss of self-confidence and a breakdown in trust. Statements such as, "I've never seen that strategy work with first graders" or "What made you think high school girls would be interested in batting averages?" are examples.

I believe that this pattern can also occur in the reverse, where the listener has already decided that anything the speaker says will be absolutely brilliant, original, and full of insight. This approach can have the same effect as a negative judgment. When the speaker believes he has nothing to prove, has already met or exceeded "the mark," creative thinking and problem solving shut down.

2. *Autobiographical listening*—Have you ever been presented with a problem or an issue that sounded so similar to your own past experience, that you began thinking about your own situation, comparing the speaker's story with your own? You associate your experience with what the speaker is saying, and the next thing you know, you're telling *your* story about what happened to *you*, instead of listening to the speaker. "You know, the same thing happened to me when I started working here. I gave parents my home contact information, and the next thing I knew, I was getting calls and emails 24/7. What I did was. . . . " This pattern is also called "highjacking" a conversation. Productive listening requires listeners to be aware of the

tendency we all have to relate similar problems or events to our own experiences. While it can be helpful for teachers to know that you understand their situation (because possibly you've experienced something similar in the past), productive listeners allow the spotlight to remain on the speaker.

3. *Inquisitive listening*—Another unproductive pattern of listening happens when the curiosity of the listener interferes with the speaker's ability to communicate their message. Many times when we are listening, we become distracted by something the speaker may say that has little to do with the main point the speaker is trying to make. We may interrupt with an irrelevant question or comment that bogs the conversation down, preventing the speaker from being heard. A teacher may want to discuss a problem he's having dealing with a difficult student. Interrupting with questions like, "Have you ever met that kid's father?" or "Did you know Angela had the same issues with him last year in sixth grade?" does not allow the teacher to say what he needs to say and feel as though he is being heard. Sometimes, teachers just need to be heard. Peppering them with questions while they are trying to speak (relevant or not) is not productive listening.

4. *Solution listening*—This is probably the most common unproductive pattern demonstrated by school leaders, because many see themselves as problem solvers. Solution listeners are eager to provide a quick and easy answer, regardless of whether they've been asked to do so! Rather than step aside and allow teachers the opportunity to solve their own problems, leaders may step in and attempt to offer solutions, *their* solutions, which, in many cases may not be the *best* solution. When leaders approach a conversation with a presumption that the teacher is competent enough to develop her own solution, they are less likely to engage in solution listening. Instead, they demonstrate respect for the teacher's capacity to think through an issue or question and to develop new ideas and alternatives that result in a better fit for both the teacher and her students.

Providing Feedback

Constructive feedback is a powerful motivator for learners. David Sousa, consultant in educational neuroscience and author of *How the Brain Learns* (2011), confirms this. In an article titled "Brain-Friendly Learning for Teachers" (2009), he shares that areas of the brain associated with motivation are more active in subjects who receive feedback during learning than those doing the same tasks without feedback. The need to be valued is a powerful emotional force. Positive feedback fills that need. Teachers who provide timely, specific feedback to students witness the effects of feedback every day. Have you ever been in a classroom when the teacher says, "I like the way Tommy raised his hand!"? Within seconds, hands pop up around the room, eagerly seeking the same response from the teacher. Feedback is a key contributor to motivation.

Feedback plays an important role in learning. Besides being a motivator, feedback provides learners with information that helps them to improve and grow. When there are clear standards of practice, feedback against those standards enables teachers to improve their performance (Danielson, 2009, p.10). To be effective, feedback must be timely and specific. Generic comments such as "Nice work," "Well planned," or "Very effective lesson," do little to improve the quality of teaching. Rather, feedback should communicate specific examples that made the lesson well planned, or very effective, such as, "Your pacing of the lesson allowed students time to reflect on their learning." This is similar to our earlier discussion about evidence. Conversations about teaching and learning are much more effective when they include specific examples based on evidence.

To increase the likelihood that desirable behaviors will continue, Sousa (2009) writes that feedback should occur as soon as possible. The sooner the teacher receives positive reinforcement about a specific strategy or behavior, the more likely the teacher is to repeat that behavior. An important point to help us remember the value of feedback is: practice does not make *perfect*; practice makes *permanent*. If we want teachers to develop effective instructional strategies and behaviors, we need to monitor their learning and provide specific and timely feedback along the way so that behaviors that become permanent are those desired behaviors that improve teaching and learning.

Facilitating Professional Goal Setting

Effective instructional leaders are able to collect evidence and assess the quality of teaching. They learn about teacher strengths and areas for growth by observing classroom practice and engaging teachers in professional conversations that reveal their understanding and thinking about teaching and learning. To improve the quality of teaching, these conversations should naturally lead to the development of professional goals. The data collected from multiple sources about the teacher's skills and understandings presents a clear picture to both teacher and supervisor about the focus for professional growth and learning. The process for developing professional goals is fully described in Chapter Four.

Once the teacher has developed a goal, the leader's role in this process is to provide guidance and support as needed. This typically means that the leader will meet with the teacher when the goal is submitted, usually at the beginning of the school year, to review the goal, clarify the intended learning outcome for the teacher, and guide any needed modifications. One of the most common adjustments needed when a teacher initially writes a goal is to help the teacher narrow his focus. Many times, teachers will write goals that are career long endeavors, such as "I will learn how to differentiate instruction." Making sure the teacher's goal is manageable makes the goal more attainable and provides opportunities for short-term wins described in Chapter Two. An example of a more manageable goal for differentiating instruction would be, "I will learn how to differentiate strategies and resources for teaching estimation to solve problems in math." This goal represents an attainable stretch within a short period of time. If the teacher is successful, she can extend the goal by applying what she's learned to other content areas. Short-term wins allow teachers to receive immediate feedback to reinforce what's working and make changes as needed along the way. During the year, the supervisor may meet with the teacher as needed to provide support, resources, and feedback.

At the end of the year, the teacher reflects on his learning and a conference is held with the supervisor, usually as part of the summative evaluation. A sample End of Year Reflection is shown in Figure 3.2. To create an appropriate balance of challenge with support requires knowing the teacher as a learner, professional, and colleague. Leaders who know their teachers will be most effective in facilitating the development and implementation of professional learning goals.

Key Points About What Leaders Need to Know

Leaders can't lead what they don't know. To improve the quality of teaching, leaders need to have certain understandings about teaching and learning. They need to spend time getting to know their teachers, as learners and professionals. Teachers don't come in one size. Knowing the way a teacher learns best, their current developmental level, and the mindset with which they approach learning enables leaders to facilitate and support teacher growth.

Leaders need to know what good teaching is. They need a clearly defined set of standards to guide their actions as instructional leaders. Without a clear picture of effective teaching, school leaders are left to play guessing games when assessing the quality of teaching.

Learning occurs when teachers are given the opportunity to be mentally active, through activities such as reflection, writing, dialogue, questioning, and collaboration with colleagues. To assess the quality of teaching in a valid and reliable way, leaders need to understand the nature of learning and provide opportunities for teachers to engage in the mental work of learning.

Leaders need to develop skills that enable them to apply these understandings and engage teachers in meaningful learning and growth. Collecting evidence of teaching through observation and conversation with teachers provide leaders with valuable information about what teachers know, understand, and are able to do. This information can be used to facilitate the growth of professional learning goals that are meaningful and manageable for teachers.

In the next chapter, we'll examine what teachers need to know in order to fully participate in their own learning and growth. For teachers to be active participants, they need knowledge and understandings that are amazingly similar to what their leaders need to know.

Putting Words Into Action

Reflecting on Your Current State

• What are some ways you get to know your staff as learners? How do you use your knowledge of staff to engage them in meaningful learning and growth? What are some examples of this?

• How do you define effective teaching? Is your definition transparent to all staff? How do you know?

Action Tools

• Evidence Anchors the Process
   o Complete the handout, *In Search of Evidence*, provided in Figure 3.3. Read each statement and determine if it is evidence or if it contains words that convey opinion, interpretation, bias, or preference. Refer to the Answer Key to check your work.

o Examine your notes from a recent observation. Refer to the description and examples of evidence provided in this chapter and the activity in Figure 3.3. What is one step you can take to improve the quality of evidence collected during a classroom visit?

Figure 3.1   Questions That Promote Reflective Thinking

About an individual lesson:

1. Compare your expectations for the lesson with how it actually went.

2. To what extent were the instructional goals met? What is the evidence of this?

3. Did you make any modifications to your plan during the lesson?

4. Describe any changes you would make if you were to teach this lesson again to the same group of students.

5. As you think about the last time you taught this lesson, what are some of the outcomes you want to have happen again?

6. When you reflect back on your lesson, what would you do differently next time you teach this lesson?

7. As you think about the results you got, what were some of the ways you designed the lesson to cause them to happen?

8. When you think about what you had planned and what actually happened, what were the similarities and what were the differences?

9. How do you think the lesson went? What happened to cause it to go that way?

10. What can the observer do to enhance your professional development?

General reflection questions:

1. What are some of the professional goals that you are working on for yourself?

2. Who or what are the resources for you as you work toward your professional goals?

3. How will you know when you're successful?

4. What was your thinking that led you to choose this strategy? Grouping? Materials? Assessment tool?

5. What did you hear (or see) that makes you think _____?

6. Give an example of what that would look like.

Figure 3.2   Teacher's End of Year Reflection

Teacher _____ **Date:** _____

The following reflection is to be shared with your evaluator in preparation for the end of year summative evaluation conference. Three essential features of professional learning are self-assessment, reflection on practice, and professional conversation. Your reflection will serve as a starting point for the End of Year Conversation, and will provide important evidence in determining the performance levels for components that are evaluated in the Summative Evaluation.

In the spaces provided below, please reflect on your professional growth for this school year. Since many professional growth experiences are related to more than one component, the reflection is organized by domains.

Please consider the following questions when writing your reflection:

In what ways did you grow as an educator?
What is the evidence of your growth?
What was the impact of your growth on student learning?

Figure 3.3   In Search of Evidence

1. _____The teacher asked a student to repeat the directions for the class.

2. _____Students are on task.

3. _____All students turned in their homework.

4. _____The students thought the lesson was boring.

5. _____The teacher smiled and greeted each student at the door as they entered.

6. _____The students at the back table were goofing off.

7. _____Teacher directions were confusing.

8. _____One student from each group put away materials.

9. _____Instructions for the activity lasted fifteen minutes.

10. _____The room arrangement is not appropriate.

Answer Key:

Evidence: 1, 3, 5, 8, 9

Opinion:

2. The key phrase here is "on task." It may be described in many ways, and is therefore not evidence. It would need to state specifically what students were doing or saying.

4. Key word is "boring." What did the students say or do to demonstrate to the observer that the lesson was boring? That would be the evidence.

6. Key phrase is "goofing off." What were students doing? Specific statements describing student actions would be evidence.

7. Key word is "confusing." What did the students do and say after directions were given? How did they demonstrate confusion?

10. Key phrase is "not appropriate." This is an interpretation and does not describe the specific room arrangement and how it impacted learning.

4

The Wisdom of Instructional Practice

What Teachers Need to Know

The best teacher is the one who NEVER forgets what it is like to be a student. The best administrator is the one who NEVER forgets what it is like to be a teacher.

Neila A. Connors (2000)

Playing a Guessing Game

When I was a teacher, I was driven by a set of beliefs, assumptions, and understandings about learning. I was guided by my belief that learners are motivated and engage when the work is meaningful, challenging, and relevant to them. I created an environment in my classroom where all students were encouraged to find their island of competence, a place where they felt confident and ready to participate in learning each and every day. I tried to get to know my students as learners, as well as people, inviting them to share personal anecdotes, accomplishments, and dreams for the future. I designed instruction by selecting materials, resources, and activities based on what I knew about my students and what I knew they needed to learn. An expectation in my classroom was that the students and I would treat each other with respect. And we regularly did.

When I was a teacher, I knew a lot of things. But I never knew if these were the *right* things, or if there were *different* things I needed to know or the district expected me to know. I had some idea what was expected of me as a teacher in the district: maintain a safe environment, be respectful of one another, communicate regularly with parents, be on time to work, attend meetings, and participate in workshops. In the classroom, what was expected of me as a teacher really depended on whom you asked. For example, we had a wonderful English Language Arts coordinator who would give me thumbs up if I was running a reader's workshop in my second-grade classroom. The science coordinator wanted to see students in groups (always in groups) with students working alongside each other to examine, predict, and discover something new. My first building principal was a stickler for routines. She liked to see a place for everything and everything in its place. I recall how impressed she was at my clothespin system for doing daily attendance and lunch count. Very efficient!

Rather than knowing what was expected of me as a teacher, I played a guessing game and made sure that each supervisor had a chance to see what I thought were the *right* things. Based on the feedback I received during my annual performance evaluation, I usually guessed right. How much more efficient and meaningful this scenario would be if, instead of playing this guessing game, teaching and professional conversations were grounded in a common understanding about what constitutes effective practice.

Guessing Games Replaced by Transparency

Understandings About Teaching and Learning

Chapter Three described essential understandings that all school leaders must have to improve the quality of teaching. They need to know and be able to recognize components of effective teaching and have a clear grasp of the standards for teaching performance. Leaders need to understand what causes learning to occur and the difference between students who are merely on task or compliant and those who are engaged in meaningful learning. As you continue reading, you'll undoubtedly notice the similarities between what leaders need to know and what teachers need to know. If we expect the quality of teaching in this country to improve, it is essential that teachers have these same understandings regarding learning and what constitutes effective practice. After all, it is the teachers who are leading the learning. Let's look at these understandings through the lens of the teacher.

First, teachers need to know how the district defines effective practice. What are the components that describe what great teachers know and do? Essentially, these components, in combination with the standards of performance, form the teacher's job description and the foundation on which they will be evaluated. I can't think of any teacher who wouldn't want to know what was expected of them each day and on what criteria they would be evaluated each year. They need to know the standard for "meeting expectations" and be able to use the levels of performance to self-assess and grow.

As mentioned in Chapter Three, many teachers complain of inconsistencies across the school and district in how expectations for performance are communicated, evaluated, and reported. When a district adopts a common set of criteria and expectations for teaching, it is essential that this information be shared with teachers. This has an immediate effect on teachers by lowering their level of concern, because expectations for teaching are no longer a guessing game. Now everyone is looking at the quality of teaching through the same transparent lens.

To develop their understanding of the teaching standards adopted by the district, teachers need opportunities to read, reflect, discuss, and share examples of these standards in action. Most teaching standards are written in generic language that enables them to be interpreted and used across a wide range of teaching, from preservice to veteran, across content areas and grade levels. Specific interpretations and examples of what the standards might look like in each classroom need to be generated by the teachers who will be demonstrating them. Let's use formative assessment as an example. If the rubric language of the standard relating to formative assessment reads, "Teacher has a well-developed strategy for using formative assessment and has designed particular approaches to be used," teachers may list strategies they use such as, thumbs up, ticket out the door, homework assignments, paired conversations, use of white boards to display student responses, and so on. These examples make the standards real and meaningful to teachers. They understand what, exactly, is expected of them for each standard and at each level of performance. When teachers understand the criteria on which their performance will be measured, they are able to reflect, self-assess, and engage in learning that is meaningful and relevant. Without this understanding, they are playing guessing games.

Teachers also need to have the same understandings as their leaders about how learning occurs and what constitutes student engagement. Learning involves active, intellectual participation on the part of the learner. Student engagement takes many forms, but always requires the learner to do the mental work. Consensus on these ideas promotes further transparency in the expectations of anyone visiting a teacher's classroom and in conversations that follow those visits. Rather than feeling they have been caught off guard, teachers know what every leader expects to see in a classroom where learning occurs. Without a common understanding of these ideas, professional conversations may become adversarial.

I recall a conversation I once had with a kindergarten teacher whose classroom I visited at the start of the day. What I observed were students who were well behaved, understood the routines of entering the classroom, putting away their things, and finding their assigned seat on the rug for the start of class. During my brief visit, students stayed put in their spot, spoke only when called on, and listened attentively to the announcements of the day. The teacher then gave directions to the whole group on how to finish assembling their Thanksgiving turkey placemats. All students proceeded to their desks on the command of the teacher, where materials needed were ready at hand. Later on, during a follow up conversation with the teacher, she raved about how "engaged" they all were during my visit. This teacher's understanding of student engagement was one of compliance, where students obediently followed the rules and routines of the classroom. Although it presented me with a valuable teachable moment, this conversation could have quickly become difficult if the stakes were high (as in a formal observation) or if there was no trust or rapport established between myself and the teacher. Conversations about student engagement and learning are more powerful (and less adversarial) when both teacher and leader have a common understanding of student engagement and are able to talk about it through the same lens!

Putting Your Know-How Into Action: A Cycle of Continuous Improvement and Growth

Once teachers have a solid understanding of the components of effective practice, the principles of learning, and of student engagement, they can begin to use this knowledge to grow and improve their practice. School leaders are better able to facilitate teacher growth when everyone is grounded in a common set of understandings and beliefs about teaching and learning. Figure 4.1 illustrates how teachers put these understandings into action by engaging in a continuous cycle of reflection, professional growth, teaching, and learning. These steps are essential to improving the quality of teaching.

The process for developing professional goals is designed to engage *the teacher in doing the mental work*. As we've already established learning is done by the learner, requiring thinking and active intellectual involvement. To begin the cycle, teachers reflect on their practice and self-assess their teaching skills. This is done using data from a number of sources. As Figure 4.2 illustrates, one of the sources of data is student learning. In addition to student learning, teachers consider feedback from their instructional leaders; building, department, or grade level initiatives; personal motivation and interests; and available resources for learning. Teachers also self-assess using the standards of teaching performance, which are usually outlined in rubric language across four to five levels. It is important to note that throughout each step in this process, school leaders are facilitating teacher learning by conducting formal and informal observations of practice and engaging teachers in professional conversations grounded in evidence of teaching and learning.

Once the teacher has completed a thorough self-assessment, he writes a goal that is stated in terms of teacher learning (rather than student learning), that is specific, measurable, and is a reasonable stretch from his current state. The teacher must also state how his learning will impact student learning. The steps in the process are strategically developed to focus squarely on teacher growth and learning. The impact on student learning is noted, but not until the teacher's goal is developed. In addition, the goal must align to one or more of the accepted teaching standards, and the teacher needs to consider potential sources of evidence that will document growth throughout the year. The steps needed for developing a Professional Learning Plan along with a template for teacher self-assessment and goal setting is shown in Figure 4.3.

As a result of this deliberate, thoughtful, and data driven assessment of practice, teachers are able to identify areas of teaching they will focus on for their own professional growth. Focusing on these areas, they are able to develop specific and strategic goals for professional learning. Providing teachers with an opportunity to reflect on their practice and to develop goals that are meaningful and relevant to their place in time is essential to teacher empowerment and growth. Bruce Marlowe and Marilyn Page wrote an article titled, "Battered Teacher Syndrome" (2000) which addressed the effects of

Figure 4.1   A Cycle of Continuous Growth and Improvement

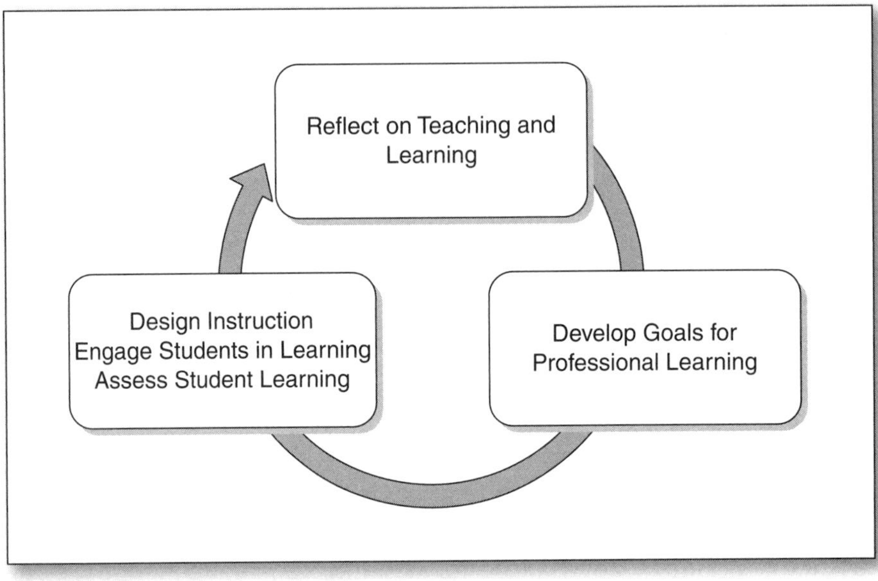

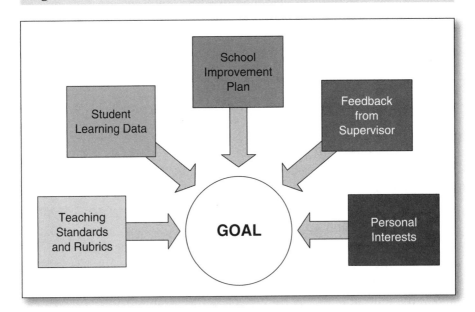

Figure 4.2   Teacher Self-Assessment: Multiple Lenses

top down mandates from the state, district, and school on teacher morale: "professional development" refers to teachers' developing professionally. It does not mean requiring teachers to accept without thinking whatever the state or district or school mandates. Do teachers currently have a clear process through which they can determine and identify their own professional needs in relation to student learning? Do they have a clear process through which they can move forward with professional goals, working with the support of their districts and their schools? (Marlowe & Page, 2000, p. 46).

This process provides teachers with an opportunity to choose goals that are meaningful and relevant to their work with students. They are more willing and motivated to engage in professional learning when given a choice and treated as professionals. It also respects the research-based knowledge about how adults learn. "Adults learn best when they are self-directed, building new knowledge upon preexisting knowledge, and aware of the relevance and personal significance of what they are learning . . . " (Croft et al., 2010, p. 8).

Once teachers have a growth plan developed, the next step is to submit it to the building leader for review and approval. This is a great opportunity for school leaders to use their professional conversation skills to facilitate a discussion about the teacher's plan for learning, as described in the previous chapter.

Following the cycle presented in Figure 4.1, the teacher's growth plan leads to teacher learning that will likely impact several components of teaching. Depending on the goals developed, the teacher may improve her ability to design differentiated instruction, raise the level of student engagement through more rigorous questions and learning activities, or implement formative assessments of student learning. Data gathered from teaching and learning will feed directly back into the teacher's reflection and subsequent growth plan.

Each of these steps represents skills and procedures that require teacher training and ongoing support from school leaders. The next section of Chapter Four will examine ways to build capacity for teacher learning within the school.

Don't Forget to Feed the Teachers!

Neila A. Connors wrote the quote that appears at the beginning of this chapter in her book titled, *If You Don't Feed the Teachers, They Eat the Students!* (2000). I couldn't agree more with this title. I believe that teaching is the most important profession there is. But I also recognize that it is one of the most challenging, which is why we must never overlook the need for teacher learning.

When a school district contacts me for consultation and professional development, it is usually to work with their leadership team. First and foremost, training and follow up support is provided to school leaders to develop their understanding of the components of effective teaching, learning, and student engagement. In addition, school leaders learn how to observe practice, evaluate teaching, and determine teaching strengths and areas for growth. The district's goal is to make sure all of the building leaders have the same understandings about teaching and learning and use the same criteria and standards for performance evaluation. However, in many cases there is no plan for teachers to develop these same understandings.

A case in point occurred several years ago when I attended a presentation at a local service agency where Charlotte Danielson was speaking about the Framework for Teaching. The Framework is used in many school districts across the country as a tool for teacher evaluation and professional growth. Sitting in the audience were the administrators from the school district where both of my children attended. As a colleague of Charlotte's and a disciple of the Framework, I initially thought how great it was that our district had developed a common understanding of teaching using the Framework. I immediately scurried over to their table excitedly saying, "I didn't know you used the Danielson Framework in your school district!" The middle school principal responded, "Yes, we do the Framework!" (Was that like the Fox Trot, or maybe the Rhumba?) When I probed him with a few questions about what steps they had taken to develop this understanding with the teachers, they looked at one another, confused as though they had misunderstood and replied, "We use the Framework, not the teachers." Apparently, the administrators had not fed the teachers!

Unfortunately, there are many more examples where administrators report that they have been using the Framework in their districts for a number of years, yet *no one* has had any training. It is no wonder why, despite ever increasing demands for improving teacher quality, much of teaching practice remains the same.

The issue of what teachers need to know about teaching and learning and how to build capacity for that understanding is absolutely essential when talking about improving the quality of teaching. We can't lead them in learning and growth if we haven't clearly communicated our expectations. We can't expect teachers to engage in reflection, to practice self-assessment, and to participate in professional conversations if they don't speak the same language. A commitment to teacher learning and a plan for teacher training must be clear and intentional.

A Plan for Teacher Learning

> In addition to gaining knowledge and
> confidence, principals have to learn to model for
> teachers the same behaviors of instruction that
> are desired within the classroom.
>
> Thomas Fowler-Finn in a conversation
> with Nancy Walser (2011)

Professional Development that builds educator effectiveness to increase student achievement applies research about learning and instructional design to achieve its intended outcomes (Walser, 2011). In other words, we need to apply what we know about effective teaching and learning to teacher learning. The design must allow teachers to understand the purpose of the learning, to be mentally active, to make connections, to recognize its relevance to their work, and to engage in reflection and collaboration with colleagues.

As a consultant working in schools around the country, it is always my recommendation that teacher learning be job embedded, with teams of educators engaged in learning through shared work. As the resident expert, I could spend days at a time training groups of teachers, using valuable (and rare) conference days or pulling them from their classrooms at the expense of the district paying for substitutes and students losing a day of instruction. Instead, we implement a systematic, job embedded plan that utilizes the talent found within the school itself. In this way, a school district builds sustainable capacity for teacher learning to continue.

This model for teacher training begins one of two ways. The first option is to invite any interested staff members and school leaders to a day of training that will include an overview of the components of professional practice, the standards for teaching performance and student engagement. After a day of training, those interested in the work may choose to become part of a district-wide training cadre. The second option is for the district to choose or invite teachers to become part of the training cadre, based on their expressed interest in the work and their demonstrated desire to lead learning with colleagues. Both options result in the formation of a team of teachers and school leaders representing every level in the district who will become trainers in each of the school buildings. Typically a building team consists of one administrators and two or three teachers.

Once the training cadre is assembled, they attend training sessions with a consultant who provides training in a mini-lesson format. The number of sessions needed depend, of course, on the available resources and the desired outcomes of the district, and the sessions may range from three to five days. One of the "Training to Lead" models that has been used in several districts includes a total of four full day sessions that are usually delivered two days at a time, spaced out during the year. Some districts opt for half day, conference day, or a summer session to limit loss of instructional time. During the first session, these future trainers participate in the training as learners, developing new understandings and skills. The goal is for members of the training cadre to know and understand the material deeply enough that they are able to teach others.

On the subsequent day, the trainers in training are given copies of leader notes and training materials and take a second walk through each lesson through the lens of a trainer. Understandings about adult learners and specific tips for presenters are shared and discussed. The future trainers are able to ask questions, clarify information presented, and anticipate possible misconceptions on the part of the learners. They have an opportunity to present an activity for their peers to practice and develop their comfort with the materials. Finally, the trainers are provided with team planning time to figure out the logistics (who, what, when, and where) for delivering these lessons in their buildings.

An important aspect of this model is that there is a clear expectation by both district and building level leaders that the delivery of the training will occur in all buildings throughout the district within a specified time frame. Having a consultant work with the training cadre periodically throughout the year allows the new trainers time to deliver the activities in their buildings in between sessions at a time and place of their choosing. The role of the building and district leadership to embed opportunities for the learning to continue throughout the year is critical to success of the model. After training sessions are completed, teachers and leaders need to apply their learning in daily conversations about teaching and learning, again and again. Unless learners practice what Blanchard, Meyer, and Ruhe (2007) call *spaced repetition*, putting learning to work through repeated practice, new learning is lost.

This model for teacher training accomplishes several desired goals. First, it taps into the human resources found within each school to facilitate teacher learning. Second, when teachers are trained to facilitate learning in their own schools, they are better able to connect with colleagues because they know the culture and can connect the learning to current initiatives. More importantly, they are invested in the work and committed to seeing it grow in their buildings. Staff members see this commitment to the work, and it raises the level of credibility to see their colleagues not only talking the talk, but walking the walk alongside them. Finally, this model builds sustainable capacity for the learning to continue as new teachers are hired, mentoring programs are developed, and as opportunities for professional conversations and peer coaching are developed in the district.

Key Points About What Teachers Need to Know

The challenge of improving the quality of teaching requires a collaborative effort by school leaders *and* teachers. It requires focus and clarity on what constitutes good teaching and how learning occurs. What teachers need to know about teaching is too important to be left up to guessing games. Teachers need to have the same understandings as their leaders so they can be actively engaged and invested in their own growth. They need to have opportunities to lead the learning and to learn from each other. Their learning needs to be spaced out over time, with brief sessions that focus on one or two essential understandings. Blanchard, Meyer, and Ruhe (2007) write:

> We need to spend ten times the amount of time following up our training as we do organizing, developing, and delivering it. We need mentors and coaches to help people move from being novices in doing what they know to becoming master teachers." (p. 103)

This chapter is about giving teachers the opportunity to become master teachers.

Chapter Five brings the big ideas presented in the previous chapters together to focus on the most powerful tool for promoting teacher growth—professional conversation. In a setting that values professional learning, with leaders and teachers who have a common vision for teaching and learning, opportunities for professional conversations that improve teacher quality abound. The next chapter demonstrates how to make the most of these opportunities.

Putting Words Into Action

Reflecting on Your Current State

- How are expectations and standards for teaching communicated to teachers?

- What opportunities are provided for teachers to engage in professional learning? Is there a common expectation across the district for teacher learning to occur?

Action Tool

Research Roundup: Defining Student Engagement

• Ask staff members to individually write their definition of student engagement. It may help to set up a hypothetical situation for them, such as, "A friend of yours has an upcoming interview with the school district for a teaching position. They want to know how to respond when they are asked about student engagement. What words or phrases come to mind in your response?"

• In small groups, ask teachers to share their responses, noting similarities and differences. Invite groups to share one or two ideas that emerged from the group conversations.

• Using one or more of the resources listed in this book, conduct a "Research Roundup." Invite teachers to read about student engagement and identify the attributes of engagement based on the research. After the reading, develop a group definition of student engagement. Compare it to the original ideas presented. How has their understanding of student engagement changed as a result of the reading and discussion?

• Apply this definition of student engagement by asking teachers to complete the handout shown in Figure 4.4.

Figure 4.3   Professional Learning Plan Development

PLP Component	Process/Tools	Outcome
Teacher Reflection and Self-Assessment	Teacher reflects using multiple sources (see attached template): Student Demographics (learning styles, cultural background, language proficiency) Student Learning Data Feedback from supervisor Curriculum/content area changes or developments School and district priorities	Teacher identifies specific areas (components) of teaching to develop, grow, and improve
Goal/Action Plan Development	Teacher develops professional learning goal and action steps	Draft of Professional Learning Goal and Action Plan developed
Meeting With Principal or Supervisor	Teacher meets with principal to review teacher professional learning goal and action plan Modifications may be made as needed Principal signs off on goal	Professional Learning Goal finalized and approved by Principal

INSTRUCTIONAL PRACTICE

SELF-ASSESSMENT

Teacher: _____   *Date:*_____

This reflection and self-assessment is the first step in developing a Professional Learning Plan. Teachers need to include multiple sources of data when reflecting on instructional practice. These sources may include the components of teaching and associated rubrics, student learning data, student demographics, curriculum changes, feedback provided by a supervisor, and school and district priorities and initiatives.

1. **What are the specific needs of my incoming students? (e.g., cultural, developmental, special needs)**
2. **How will changes in the curriculum or developments in my content area impact my planning, teaching, or assessment of student learning?**
3. **What building or district priorities or goals will impact my teaching?**
4. **In what areas of teaching do I excel? What are some areas with room for growth?**
5. **Based on your self-assessment, are you ready to develop a professional goal? If not, what other information do you need? (student learning data, district, department, grade level priorities, and so on)**

Teacher:

_____

Building/Department:

_____
_____

Supervisor:

_____

Title:

_____

1. **PROFESSIONAL GOAL: What is your professional learning goal? What are you intending to learn?**

2. **TEACHING: Which teaching standards or components of practice does this goal address?**

3. **STUDENT LEARNING: How will this goal impact student learning?**

4. **EVIDENCE: What evidence will you collect to document the progress of this goal?**

Quantitative Evidence:

Qualitative Evidence:

List below the steps needed to implement this goal.

#	Action Steps	Timeline	Resources Needed	Benchmark(s) (Indicators of Completion)
1				
2				
3				
4				
5				

Teacher:

_____

Building/Department:

_____

_____

Supervisor: _____

_____

Title: _____

_____

1. PROFESSIONAL GOAL: What is your professional learning goal? What are you intending to learn?

Improve strategies for developing high level questions and increasing rigor for all students in class discussions and student work.

2. TEACHING: Which teaching standards or components of practice does this goal address?

State Standards II.5, III.1, II.1,2,5, I.1,3,5

_-or-_

1a: Demonstrating knowledge of content*
1b: Demonstrating knowledge of students*
3c: Engaging students in learning*
3b: Using questioning and discussion techniques*

*Framework for Teaching components of practice

3. STUDENT LEARNING: How will this goal impact student learning?

Increase the level of student participation in class discussions.

Increase the level of thinking and reflection in student responses (written and verbal)

4. EVIDENCE: What evidence will you collect to document the progress of this goal?

Quantitative Evidence:
Student assessment results
Student writing samples
Qualitative Evidence:
Teacher observation
Anecdotal records/chart/log
Student reflections
Teacher reflections

Teacher signature: _____

Administrator signature: _____

Figure 4.4   Understanding Student Engagement

What are the signs of student engagement in your classroom? What do you look for? How do you support student engagement in learning? List specific examples in the spaces below.

What would students be doing/saying?	What would teachers be doing/saying to support students?

5

Promoting Teacher Learning

It's All Talk!

Of all the approaches available to educators to promote teacher learning, the most powerful (and embedded in virtually all others) is that of professional conversation.

Charlotte Danielson (2009)

Powerful Conversations

In a book intended to provide a laser-like focus on improving teacher quality, no topic can be of more importance than professional conversations. My experiences with educators across the country has convinced me that Danielson was right in declaring professional conversations to be the most powerful approach to teacher learning. By the way, it's also the *least expensive* way. Schools today are populated with teacher talent. Professional conversations among trained educators tap this valuable resource, providing limitless opportunities for learning and growth. Provided, that is, that those engaged in conversation understand a few things.

Let's begin with a teacher's reflection on the power of professional conversations. Lynda Courage is a veteran teacher who served on a committee to redesign her district's teacher evaluation system. Her work on the committee gave her the opportunity to engage in professional conversations, using the language of Danielson's Framework for Teaching. After participating in a series of informal classroom visits designed to model the power of professional conversation, Lynda decided to try this process out for herself. She shared her experience:

> As part of my work on the district teacher evaluation committee, I took part in a series of informal classroom visits with several of my colleagues. It was a great opportunity to see my coworkers in action through the lens of the Framework. In between each visit, we met and discussed what we observed. Our visits were based on the assumption that even good teachers have room for growth and, as we learned, "You don't have to be bad to get better." That statement stuck with me throughout the day as I visited classrooms and we engaged in conversation about what we had seen and heard. Although pre-observation conferences were not required in our district, I decided that, for my upcoming annual observation, I would request a meeting with the building principal to talk about my plan using the Framework language and the forms we had developed for our district. Rarely do I seek out an administrator for an extra meeting, but I was excited to try a new approach was encouraged by my principal's enthusiastic response to my request.
>
> I used the pre-observation form to organize my thinking about the lesson I was going to teach. I felt like I was taking charge of my professional development by identifying places in my lesson where I wanted my principal to focus and provide me with feedback. Our pre-observation conference was a pivotal growth piece in my professional learning. I was able to set a context based on where I had been with instruction, what I wanted students to learn that day, and how I hoped the learning would continue after the observation. It was an opportunity for two professionals to share a great conversation about teaching. I wanted feedback to make the lesson better—it was a good lesson, but I wanted to breathe life into it. My principal had an understanding of what I wanted to do and was willing to assist me in further developing the positive process of the lesson.

Our post observation discussion revolved around the points I had asked her to focus on during our pre-observation. As a result, I was able to identify areas I wanted to improve upon. We had a great collegial conversation about my lesson which was guided by a common language and clear expectations. It was a team effort focused on my professional learning needs. I felt like I had a major role in my own professional development. (L.Courage, personal communication, April 19, 2012)

The conversation that took place between Lynda and her principal was the result of deliberate and intentional actions taken by both teacher and school leader. How does a leader set the stage for conversations that impact teaching to occur?

Setting the Stage

Acknowledging the Leader's Dual Role

What are the prerequisite conditions necessary for engaging in powerful conversations that improve teaching and learning? The first four chapters of this book have laid a foundation by presenting the essential conditions, knowledge, and skills that are needed by school leaders. These conditions set the stage for powerful conversations. In Chapter Two, we described the importance of establishing a culture for learning where all teachers expect that their teaching will be questioned and explored by colleagues and supervisors, not because there's anything wrong with their teaching, but because teaching is so complex that it requires continuous growth and change. We established, in Chapter Three, that successful school leaders possess essential understandings about teaching and learning and use certain skills to engage teachers in learning and continuous growth.

For conversations to reach their maximum potential, however, school leaders must also understand what Danielson (2009) calls the "dual nature" of leadership in professional organizations. That is, school leaders actually have two, somewhat conflicting roles to play. First, they have what can be referred to as hierarchical or positional authority over teachers. They make the decisions that impact teacher retention; they administer evaluations; they are considered *the boss*. On the other hand, school leaders also have the job of leading professionals, many of whom have experience and understanding that extends beyond that of their *boss*. Let's consider how the reality of this dual role impacts the way school leaders talk with teachers.

We've established that school leaders are not (nor would it be reasonable to expect they would be) experts in all content areas and grade levels. Some school leaders enter their role with extensive backgrounds and skills focused on a particular content area or grade level. Others bring limited experience in teaching and learning to their supervisory position. As such, one would expect that many teachers have deeper knowledge about what (and whom) they teach than their principals. This reality creates a tension for leaders that requires a careful balance between their positional authority and the realities of leading a group of professionals. Let's take the example of a high school principal whose background is music. Although he may know the difference between an interlude and an intermission, he may not be able to distinguish between the processes of meiosis and mitosis. He doesn't know a transitive from an intransitive verb. He may think the Battle of the Bulge is part of the new Health curriculum. And yet, *he* will ultimately assign a label, indicating the proficiency level of the biology teacher, the English teacher, and the history teacher. Although some may view this paradox as a potential problem, it actually provides rich soil for cultivating powerful conversations.

This new paradigm for the role of school leaders should be viewed as good news. When leaders acknowledge the dual nature of their role and accept that they don't need to have all of the answers, they open the door for meaningful dialogue with teachers. In the past, leaders were expected to have all the answers, to advise, and to direct teachers with suggestions and mandates. As any principal will admit, this was not a realistic expectation, even for the most seasoned instructional leader. However, if we accept the role of the instructional leader as one who guides, coaches, and mentors teachers by listening and asking questions that help teachers find the answers, then the principal is no longer the sage on the stage, but a trusted guide on the side.

Cheliotes and Reilly in their book, *Coaching Conversations*, summarize the benefits of this approach to instructional leadership:

> This kind of leadership taps into the thinking and passions of others by seeking to develop the strengths and interests of others. It is not one person who determines success; it is the group that creates success. This engenders a culture of continuous improvement for all and a *shared* pride in achievements."
> (2010, p. 12)

When a school and district develop common understandings about teaching and learning and view the role of the school leader as a facilitator rather than a director of learning, there is tremendous potential for powerful conversations among educators that improve instructional practice.

Making Intentions Clear

A critical first step in designing instruction for students is to determine the intended learning outcome. This is also true when leading professional conversations. The intent and purpose of the conversation must be clear to both leaders and teachers. Consider the brief, unannounced classroom visit. These visits provide rich information that serve as the basis for productive conversations with teachers. However, in most cases these visits become lost opportunities to engage teachers in reflection and growth. One reason for this is the lack of transparency in purpose and expectations around unannounced visits.

Think about the visits made to classrooms by leaders in your building and district. Are they conducted in your school on a regular basis? Are the visits guided by a district or building protocol, such as Instructional Rounds (City, Elmore, Fiarman, & Teitel, 2009) or the Three Minute Classroom Walkthrough (Downey, Steffy, Fenwick, Frase, & Poston, 2004)? Or are they more impromptu, occurring when you find yourself with an hour to spare? Do you use a checklist or a "problem of practice" to guide these brief visits? Or do you fly by the seat of your pants when sticking your head into a classroom for five minutes? Why do you visit classrooms? To be visible to teachers and students? To collect data about the use of a strategy or resource? To check up on teachers you are concerned about? To get to know teachers and students? To improve instruction and learning? All of the above?

If you are an instructional leader, you probably have an answer to all of these questions. But if you ask a teacher the same questions, would *they* know the answers? Most teachers will say their leaders do make periodic, unannounced visits to their classrooms. Although the frequency of impromptu visits varies in each school, most teachers will also say that they are unclear of the purpose behind these visits. They may guess that the principal wants to get to know the students, become more familiar with the staff because they are new to the building, or maybe would rather be out and about than to face the paperwork sitting on her desk!

The important point is that most teachers don't know the purpose, nor do they recall learning anything new as a result of these visits. Aside from a note left in their mailbox the next day ("It was great visiting your class today. Keep up the good work!"), they receive virtually no feedback or engage in any conversations with the school leader about their lesson. If teachers don't know the intent of the visits and don't realize any value in them, it's understandable why many prefer to keep their doors closed or may be on edge when the principal drops by their classroom unannounced.

The exception to this scenario happens in schools where they've created a synergy based on common beliefs and understandings about teaching and learning. In a school that has developed a common understanding about the components of effective teaching, teachers are clear about what leaders may be looking for when they enter the classroom. When leaders establish and communicate that their purpose for classroom visits is to explore and extend thinking, reflect on practice, generate new ideas, problem solve, and analyze data collected from student learning, teachers expect the conversations that follow these visits to be meaningful and worthwhile. The first step in having meaningful conversations is to replace guessing games by making intentions clear. Maryann Fletcher, principal of a suburban middle school, shares her experience working with a history teacher:

> Working with veteran staff in a secondary school around instruction poses many challenges. As a building level administrator I have often struggled with my grasp of some content areas when functioning in the role of instructional leadership. The use of the Framework for Teaching has provided me with tools that have enabled me to help members of my staff refine instruction in a way that has served to help transform work in classrooms. The common language of the Framework and the materials in the toolkit Implementing the Framework for Teaching (2009) have helped me hone my craft to serve the teachers—and their students—in a more thoughtful and coherent manner.
>
> I have a Social Studies teacher in my school who is the master of storytelling. He has a large repertoire of material and students always report enjoying his class. But the question he was starting to ask himself had to do with how engaged his students were and how could he change his practices to increase their engagement. He is an experienced teacher who had sought out the challenge of a different grade level as a means of changing his approach but found that it was difficult to move away from the stories he loved. Recently,

he came to a pre-observation meeting with some ideas about an upcoming lesson that was not fully formed. In a typical observation cycle, this "lack of preparation" would be seen in a negative light. Instead, it signaled an opportunity to have a collegial conversation that is the hallmark of our new approach to teacher learning.

He was embarking on a unit on the American Revolution, and he wanted to address the growing discontent with and protest of the colonists with the rules and governance of England. He wanted his observation to focus on two specific areas of the lesson: questioning and discussion strategies and student engagement in learning. We started by looking at the levels of teaching performance in each of these areas so we were both clear about expectations. We brainstormed ideas off the central theme and discussed how he would use a video clip from the HBO series, *John Adams.*

The postobservation conversation was very powerful; he identified some strengths of the lesson and was able to identify some places for growth. Our discussion was very reflective, focused on the evidence of teaching and learning collected during the lesson and samples of student work. Having established a common language to talk about teaching allowed both the teacher and me to share in a deep discussion about the lesson, the student learning, and his ongoing effort to change the paradigm of teacher directed lessons. The period passed quickly, and we were both struck by the bell—the conversation had not ended but the period had. (M. Fletcher, personal communication, April 17, 2012)

Factors That Impact Conversations

Conversations are not created equal. Professional conversations take many paths and detours along the road. The path of any conversation is dependent on a number of factors. These are the same factors that impact success with students in the classroom, so educators should be very familiar with each one. It's interesting to note that when we think about how to engage in meaningful conversations with adults, many of us forget to think about what we already know about conversations with students. This relationship is analogous. Think of a conversation you've had with a colleague that went well; it may have turned up some new ideas, developed an alternative way to approach a problem, or identified additional resources to support teaching and learning. These are the conversations we strive for, those that impact teaching by adding to a teacher's toolkit and simultaneously building trust and confidence in the process itself.

Rapport and Relationship With the Teacher

Some would argue that the most important factor that impacts the success of a conversation is the level of trust and rapport that exist between the teacher and supervisor. Without trust, teachers are unwilling to take the risks needed to engage in honest reflection and dialogue about their practice. If a teacher has *been burned* by an administrator in the past, or felt she was unfairly treated or misunderstood, then her *wall* is up, the shades are pulled down tight and the "Do Not Enter" sign is clearly in view. We can all picture a teacher–supervisor relationship that bears these signs. The only conversations likely to happen in this case are adversarial.

How can a leader begin to repair trust that has been broken with a teacher? I can think of many ways that we've already mentioned. Communicating expectations and purpose with transparency (rather than guessing games) is essential. Using a common language that the teacher can interpret in his own context is another important tool. I would never ask a teacher to describe how he engaged students in learning unless I knew the teacher and I had developed a common understanding of the term "student engagement."

Another tool we've discussed is creating short-term wins. To create short-term wins for the teacher, find her *islands of competence* and begin conversations by recognizing and celebrating what she does well. Comment on her effective teaching strategies, on how she deals with difficult students, or on her organizational skills—pick something and point it out to the teacher. Follow up with questions that respect the teacher's experience and developmental level, that serve to challenge her thinking without undermining her confidence. This demonstrates professional respect for the teacher by communicating, "I know you are capable. I want to hear your ideas."

In a culture that respects the school history, with common beliefs and understandings about expectations for teaching in place, teachers feel safe to take risks and expose their vulnerabilities. In a culture where "you don't have to be bad to get better," teachers expect to engage in conversations that question their practice and push at the margins of their thinking. Establishing trust is a precondition for learning and growth to occur, with students as well as teachers.

The Developmental Level of the Teacher

The conversation a school leader has with a competent veteran teacher follows a different path and is guided by different assumptions than a conversation with a teacher who is struggling or may be new to the profession. When trust and rapport are established, experienced teachers are able to engage in thinking and generate their own ideas, drawing from a *teaching toolbox* that has been developed over many years. Teachers who are new to the profession are also able to think deeply about instructional decisions but pull ideas from a few basic tools rather than the whole hardware store. Analogous to the conversations we have with students, questions to teachers must be asked at their *just right* level. School leaders need to consider and respect what the teacher knows (and doesn't know) when framing a question to a teacher. The same question that seems condescending to an experienced teacher may intimidate his novice counterpart. We never want to ask questions or engage teachers in conversations that back them into a corner where they are unable to find a safe way out.

School leaders need to consider the assumptions that are embedded in every question they ask. For example, the question, "How do you differentiate questions to students that reflect their abilities?" contains a number of assumptions. First, it assumes the teacher knows the students' ability levels, and uses this information to differentiate questions posed to students. It further assumes that the teacher has the knowledge and resources needed to ask a range of questions on a given topic. Asking this question of a novice teacher whose teaching style is predominantly *one size fits all* would not be starting the conversation at that teacher's *just right* level. The purpose of these conversations is to promote teacher learning and growth. Instead, a leader might ask this teacher, "What do you need to know about your students to ask questions that are at their 'just right' level?" School leaders need to know their teachers' developmental level and apply the principles of learning to the feedback, suggestions, and questions they present when talking to teachers.

The School Culture

Much has already been said about the importance of creating a culture for professional learning to occur. A leader who demonstrates the core beliefs of the school each day in their deeds and actions with teachers, students, support staff, and parents has taken the first step in creating a context for meaningful conversations to occur among teachers. When teachers see their leaders spending time in classrooms, participating in professional learning alongside them, offering help and guidance to a teacher struggling with a difficult student or parent, or obtaining needed resources to support teaching and learning, they begin to recognize their own role in demonstrating the core beliefs of the school. This creates a powerful synergy between teachers and leaders.

Embedded in every culture are norms that govern accepted behavior. In a culture where leaders have always done the mental work and teachers have skated by without doing any thinking (hence, any learning), teachers respond with concern and alarm when leaders pose questions about their teaching. "I don't know! Why are you asking me? Isn't it *your* job to just tell me what I'm supposed to do next?" Or, "Why are you asking me to explain *why* I used that strategy. . . . did I do something wrong?" Teachers who are used to sitting and listening while their leader tells them about their teaching are caught off guard when asked to think and reflect.

This is why Chapter Five comes *after* Chapters One through Four—a school leader can't put his teachers in the driver's seat and expect them to safely drive the car without first laying the foundation and developing understandings for them to have a safe trip. Leaders *and* teachers need to develop similar understandings and skills described in previous chapters. They each need to understand their role in improving practice. The school culture shapes the norms that impact the path of each and every conversation.

The Data Collected About Teaching and Learning

Another factor that impacts conversations is the information or data about teaching and learning that is collected from classroom visits and artifacts of teaching and learning. This rich data provides the leader with necessary talking points for the conversation. Consider how data about learning guides our conversations with students. Teachers use evidence of learning to determine how to respond to student questions, guide their thinking, provide additional resources or opportunities for practice, adjust the pace of instruction, and so on. School leaders use teaching data in much the same way. Ten minutes in a teacher's classroom provides many data points that can be used to guide a follow up conversation with the teacher. Teacher statements, student behavior, resources used, pacing of the lesson, and student work samples are among the many sources of information that is collected in a classroom. This data helps leaders determine the teacher's *just right* level for engaging in a conversation with the teacher that is intellectually challenging, without undermining her confidence.

Is there a particular type of data that fuels powerful conversations about teaching and learning? Most certainly there is: data that relates to *transparent*, agreed-upon standards and expectations for teaching and learning; and data that is based on evidence of teaching, rather than bias or interpretation. Before talking with teachers, examine the data. What does it tell you? How will you use this data to begin a conversation with the teacher? Later on in this chapter, we provide a list of topics that can help leaders determine what type of data to collect and discuss.

The Teacher's Mindset

Chapters Two and Three highlighted the importance of understanding mindset for both leaders and teachers. A teacher's view of intelligence impacts how they respond in conversations that question them and push their thinking to new levels. Teachers with a growth mindset regard conversations as opportunities to learn and grow. They are motivated by challenging conversations that provide intellectual stimulation. They are eager to respond to questions, and they approach conversations with an expectation to learn something new.

Teachers whose view of intelligence is fixed may feel threatened by questions about their teaching. They are comfortable with the status quo and would rather be left alone than place their intellect under scrutiny. These teachers are easy to spot in a conversation. They communicate through nonverbal cues such as posture and facial expressions that say, "I've been teaching for twenty years. What could I possibly need to learn now? If it's not broken, don't fix it! How long is this going to take?"

Leaders need to recognize the impact that mindset has on professional conversations. Many times leaders may misinterpret a teacher's reluctance to engage in thoughtful reflection and conversation, thinking it relates to their relationship with the teacher. The reality is that many teachers resist engaging in conversations not because they don't like the person asking the questions, but because they feel threatened by the conversation or they may view conversations as a waste of time because conversations have never been meaningful or worthwhile before. Acknowledging the role that a teacher's mindset plays in a professional conversation helps school leaders better understand how to connect with teachers in meaningful ways.

The Skills of the Leader Facilitating the Conversation

In Chapter Three, we examined the skill set necessary for leaders to engage in professional conversations with teachers. They need to be able to ask questions that promote reflection and extend the teacher's thinking. They need to employ productive listening skills, focusing their attention squarely on the teacher's learning needs. Finally, leaders need to provide timely, specific feedback that helps teachers grow and learn and encourages them to repeat strategies that are working.

The leader's expertise in using these skills has a direct impact on the path a conversation follows. If a leader speaks to a competent veteran teacher using a direct, top down approach, the potential to engage the teacher in reflection and dialogue is greatly reduced. Rather than contributing to the conversation by sharing ideas, the teacher will politely sit, appearing to listen, while wondering how much more time this "conversation" will take.

Asking teachers questions that have obvious answers, "Did you have enough supplies available?" or making suggestions that reflect the leader's own bias or experiences, will also lead to a one-sided conversation. Saying to a teacher "I had trouble getting kids to read independently. You might try rewarding them for reading. They can earn points towards a pizza party. That worked for my students," does little to invite thinking or resolve the issue for that teacher in that circumstance. However, that same conversation will take an entirely different path when the leader is skilled at listening and asking questions that invite the teacher to think and problem solve. Questions such as, "What are some ways you could encourage students to choose independent reading during free time?" or "What skills would students need to have to be able to make good choices for independent reading?" encourages the teacher to consider ways to approach the issue of independent reading. This approach doesn't imply judgment or criticism of the teacher; however, it does require the *teacher* to develop some ideas of his own. Not only will this promote teacher learning by engaging him in thinking, it also communicates respect for the teacher's intellect.

All teachers and leaders have strengths in certain conversation skills while others need work. Someone once pointed out that we have two ears and one mouth, so we should listen twice as much as we talk. This is a reminder that serves me well as I continue to develop my own listening skills. School leaders need to reflect on their skill set and continue to practice and develop those skills that will engage teachers in learning and growth.

Leading Conversations: When, What, and How

When to Talk

Throughout the school day, leaders have many opportunities to talk with teachers. Informal conversations occur throughout the day as teachers enter and leave the school building, grab their mail from the office, stop for coffee in the faculty room, or pass by in the hallway. These are typically *congenial* conversations that serve as opportunities to develop rapport and set a positive tone in the school environment. Rick DuFour (2003) uses the term "collaboration lite" to refer to these informal get-togethers, such as holiday parties, baby showers, and softball games, where the conversations are generally congenial. Informal conversations are an important part of the school culture, but they don't improve teacher quality.

Conversations that promote teacher learning are more *collegial* in nature and are focused on topics of teaching and learning. They may be formal, as in a scheduled pre-observation conference, or informal, as in the conversations that take place among groups during a workshop or collegial circle. Their purpose is to improve teaching and learning. It is important to make this distinction because school and district leaders often have different ideas about what constitutes professional, collegial work. Conversations that improve teaching and learning are grounded in a common understanding about effective practice and evidence of student learning.

Observing instructional practice is one of the most direct tools a principal has to collect evidence that enables them to engage in collegial conversations. Most observations in schools today are conducted as formal observations, in the sense that they are scheduled with advance notice to the teacher, last an entire class period, and may include a preconference, postconference, or both.

Brief, informal observations also provide an opportunity for leaders to engage in collegial conversations. These visits are usually unannounced and, depending on the process used, may last from five to fifteen minutes. Although these brief, informal classroom visits are conducted for a number of reasons in schools today (to gather trend data, to be visible in the building, to check on the use of a newly purchased instructional resource, such as technology or curriculum materials), few leaders use these visits as an opportunity to improve instruction by talking with teachers.

A recent study published in the Journal of Educational Administration (Ing, 2010) examined the impact of informal observations by the school leader on improving instruction. The researchers found that even frequent, informal visits are unlikely to improve instruction unless they are followed up with a conversation with the teacher about what was observed.

We've established the important role of feedback in learning. Feedback motivates learners to repeat desired behaviors and provides specific information that helps them improve and grow. Time consuming classroom walkthroughs represent time lost if they aren't followed by conversations with teachers. To improve the quality of teaching, principals need to have a better understanding of what to talk about and a process for engaging teachers in professional conversations that follow a classroom observation.

What to Talk About

I have accompanied many school leaders on classroom visits to practice collecting evidence of teaching and learning. Before entering the teacher's classroom, they'll frequently ask, "What should I be looking for? How will I know if I'm looking at the right things?" There is so much to see and hear in a classroom, even for a brief, ten minute visit, that observation can seem overwhelming unless we have a plan. Fortunately, in a school that has established a common understanding of effective teaching among both leaders and teachers, what to talk about is clearly defined. Agreed upon teaching standards provide a guide or map for leaders to use when deciding what to look for and what to talk about with teachers.

Charlotte Danielson's book, *Talk About Teaching* (2009) provides topics of conversation that help guide the collection of evidence when visiting a classroom and the conversations that follow. The topics were developed based on Danielson's *Framework for Teaching* (ASCD, 2007), a widely used and accepted instrument for teacher evaluation, growth, and development. Regardless of whether a school uses the Framework, these topics are relevant and essential to any classroom setting. Table 5.1 provides a list of the topics, along with guiding questions for the observer. The questions reflect what an observer might be asking himself when visiting the classroom. Considering these questions helps the observer to focus on specific aspects of teaching and learning.

School leaders and teachers find this guide to be a useful tool to help manage all of the data that is available when visiting a classroom. Leaders comment that it helps them focus on a particular component of teaching by using the questions to guide what they are looking to see and hear. Who is doing the mental work, the teacher or the students? How do you know? What are students learning? Can students articulate what they are learning? Does the task or activity require the students to think?

All students? The answers to these questions provide the data points that serve as a starting point in a collegial conversation.

Teachers who have participated in classroom visits using the topics of conversation as a tool comment that they like using the guide because it provides consistency in what is looked at in a teacher's classroom. It is important to mention that if a school chooses to use a guide such as the Topics listed in Table 5.1, they need to share this with the teachers. This Topics list is another tool for promoting transparency in communicating expectations to teachers. Making use of the list is analogous to what we ask of teachers, that they make expectations for learning clear to students.

It is also important to note that the topics of conversation differ from a checklist of teacher behaviors, which may be manageable for the observer to use but lacks any meaningful feedback for the teacher. A guide such as the Topics list helps make the task of collecting evidence both manageable and meaningful for observers. Many checklists lack validity and lend themselves to misinterpretation simply because they do not require evidence and are subject to observer bias. To promote reliability and reduce bias, observers need to read, discuss, and understand each of the topics of conversation. Before observing in classrooms, learners will frequently practice together in small groups, collecting evidence using case studies and videotapes of teaching. Monthly leadership meetings that are dedicated to group practice and collegial conversations help leaders develop the confidence and skills needed to engage teachers in learning and growth.

How to Talk

How can school leaders use the evidence collected during a classroom visit in a way that promotes teacher learning and growth? Let's describe the setting in which powerful conversations occur. First, the school leader collects evidence using a clear lens, absent of any rose-colored glasses. The school itself is a place where reflection on practice and collegial conversations are viewed as opportunities to grow and learn. Standards for professional practice are communicated and understood by both teachers and school leaders. Procedures and their purposes are transparent. Teachers expect to learn by engaging in thoughtful conversations and rely on their leaders to listen and ask questions that push at the margins of the teachers' understanding and skill levels. Teachers and leaders are ready to talk about teaching and learning.

The following protocol can be used to begin professional conversations following a brief, informal classroom visit or as a way to begin a postobservation conference. This process has been implemented by

Table 5.1 Topics for Conversation

Guiding Questions	
Topic	*Questions to Consider*
Clarity of purpose	What are the students learning? How do you know? How is the learning outcome communicated to students? What connections does the teacher make between today's learning and either previous or upcoming learning?
Rigorous learning tasks and assignments	Does the task pose a problem or challenge to solve? Describe. To what degree are they able to make choices and be self-directed in their learning? What is the level of cognitive challenge? How is the task differentiated to promote rigor and cognitive engagement for all students? Are students able to move to the next level when they are ready to do so?
High levels of energy and student engagement	What are the students doing? What are they saying? If they are working in groups, are all students participating? Do the tasks demand higher level thinking? Do students initiate improvements in their work? Have students "bought into" the work at hand? How do you know? Who is doing the mental work in the classroom? The teacher, or the students? All students? How do you know?
A safe and challenging environment	What is the nature of the interactions between teacher and students? Among students? How does the teacher show respect for each student's intellect? How does the teacher convey the importance of the learning to students? Is the environment a safe one for students to take risks? How do you know?
Smooth organization and management	To what extent are the routines and procedures effective? How do you know? Do students play a role in carrying out the routines? Do they know where materials are located? Can they move from one place to another without incident? How do routines and procedures impact the use of instructional time?
Implementation of school or district initiatives	Are the school or district initiatives evident in the classroom? What is the evidence of this? What impact are the initiatives having on student learning? How do you know?

Source: Topics adapted from *Topics of Conversation* by Charlotte Danielson, *Talk About Teaching!*. Corwin, 2009.

district, building, and teacher leaders as a way to engage teachers in conversation and extend their thinking about the events of a learning experience observed in their classroom. It is based on the topics of conversation presented earlier. However, any set of teaching standards can be used in their place, provided, of course that both teachers and school leaders understand their meaning.

The rules for providing effective feedback apply here. First, it must relate to one or more of the topics of conversation or agreed upon teaching standards. Second, feedback should be timely, specific, and constructive. The closer the conversation occurs to the actual events in the classroom, the more meaningful the conversation will be. It is also recommended that the conversation occur in the teacher's setting, usually her classroom, rather than in the principal's office. This sets a more collaborative tone and allows the teacher to readily access relevant materials and resources as a reference during the conversation.

The process begins when the leader collects evidence during a classroom visit. The leader uses the topics of conversation to guide his thinking and observations. During a brief visit, it is more important to observe and listen than to take notes as you may do during a formal observation. As the events of the lesson unfold, the observer determines which topics of conversation are most relevant. For example, when I am in a classroom for any length of time, the first thing I look for is the learning outcome. I frequently find myself wondering what the students are learning because it may not be apparent during my visit. This may be the topic I choose to focus on during my conversation with the teacher. If the learning outcome is clear, I look for evidence of student thinking. What are the students doing? Does the task present a challenge or require higher levels of thinking? The questions listed in Table 5.1 represent the script that is running in my head while I am in the classroom. These questions help determine where to begin the follow up conversation with the teacher.

After the visit, the leader meets with the teacher and begins the conversation. A three step process for conducting this conversation is described below.

1.   Begin with a positive statement regarding something you saw or heard. This is your opportunity to celebrate the teacher's islands of competence and verbally recognize what's working with the teacher. The statement may reference any of the topics of conversation such as the environment, the energy and excitement of the students, or the teacher's organization and management of the class. It may include something *you* learned from the lesson, such as an instructional strategy, an interesting fact, a new skill, or even a creative way to handle a noninstructional routine such as taking attendance.

2.   The next step opens the door to the topic, by restating something you observed. This is a critical step that many leaders unknowingly omit when talking to teachers. They jump right to the question, without opening the door. Consider this example. If a leader asks a teacher, "What are some ways you can check for student understanding after giving directions for an activity?" the teacher may not see the relevance in the question and wonder what the leader is after. However, if the question is preceded by a statement such as, "I noticed several students began the experiment without getting the right materials," the teacher understands the relevance and meaning of the question. This is also an opportunity to provide information that guides the teacher's thinking. In this example, the leader may add, "When students are following a new procedure, they typically need to review the directions before getting started. Knowing that not all students are auditory learners, what are some other ways to provide students access to the directions for the activity?"

3.   The final step is to ask a question that invites the teacher to think about a topic of conversation. The question should not assign judgment, but invite additional information and thinking that clarifies the events observed in the classroom. Leaders who know their teachers are able ask questions at the *just right* level in a way that respects teachers' level of expertise and confidence. When questions are asked following a brief, unannounced visit, it is critical to refrain from making a final judgment before talking with the teacher. If evidence was gathered without context, there are likely to be many gaps that need to be filled in before a complete picture is formed.

The following example illustrates the three step process for beginning a conversation after a classroom visit.

During the visit

Although the teacher encouraged students to work with a partner or in small groups, all students were completing the same task, answering a list of questions (generated by the teacher) regarding the video the class watched together. Several groups finished the task early, and three students needed teacher assistance to complete the task.

Three-Step Conversation Strategy

1.   It's obvious that you've developed an environment where students are respectful of one another when working in small groups and know the routines for working together on a task. Students

readily knew where to get materials and took turns answering the questions on the handout.

2.   I noticed that after watching the video, all students were completing the same assignment, answering a list of questions you had generated. Some of the students whipped right through the handout, and others needed your help. With such a wide range of student abilities in your class, I'm sure it's a challenge to meet all of their needs.

3.   How might this activity be modified in the future to address the learning needs of all students?

The question posed to this teacher makes the assumption that the teacher has some ideas about ways to modify the activity. Rather than lead the teacher by providing suggestions, the question invites the teacher to consider other ways for students to respond to the video. The teacher's response will direct the leader to the next question. If the teacher gets stuck, the leader may "feed" the teacher with additional information to guide his thinking. It is important for leaders to begin with a question that respects the teacher's intellect without undermining his confidence.

You may be wondering how long these conversations take. As is true in all learning, it depends on the goal. The length of the conversation should be guided by the desired outcome. If we apply what we know about learning, less is more. It is much more meaningful (and manageable) to focus on one key point or big idea for ten minutes than to overwhelm the teacher with a thirty-minute recitation of points to ponder. The goal is teacher learning, one step at a time.

Key Points About Promoting Teacher Learning

Professional conversation is the most powerful tool for school leaders to improve the quality of teaching. Collegial conversations that focus on standards of practice engage teachers in reflection and dialogue that promote learning. Conversations are most effective when school leaders recognize their role as a facilitator rather than the director of teacher thinking.

Conversations follow many different paths, depending on a number of important factors. The school culture, the developmental level of the teacher, and the relationship that exists between the teacher and the school leader impact the direction a conversation takes. The teacher's mindset and openness to learning play a pivotal role in how willing they are to engage in conversations that raise questions about their teaching.

Powerful conversations also rely on a leader's skill in collecting evidence, choosing a topic to begin the conversation, forming questions at the teacher's *just right* level and listening to the teacher's response.

Both formal and informal classroom visits present an opportunity for the leader to improve instruction when the visits are followed by a conversation with the teacher. Using a three step protocol, the conversations focus on topics of teaching and learning that recognize positive attributes of teaching but also raise questions that extend the teacher's thinking and repertoire of strategies. This strategy engenders a culture of professional learning that puts teachers squarely in the driver's seat.

It is well known that learning occurs through active participation and mental engagement by the learner. Learning to lead meaningful professional conversations occurs when the learner has opportunities to talk about teaching and applies the skills and understandings presented in this chapter. Professional learning—it's all talk!

The first five chapters have mainly referenced *school* leaders such as building principals as key to improving teacher quality. However, the district office plays a pivotal role in hiring and cultivating principals who are instructional leaders. In the same way that teachers rely on school leaders to flourish and grow, building principals rely on a central office that shares the same vision and beliefs. The next chapter focuses on the role of the district office in improving teacher quality.

Putting Words Into Action

Reflect on Your Current State

- Think about a time when you've faced an important issue in your role as a leader. How did you problem solve? What strategies helped facilitate your thinking? Did you seek the counsel of an experienced colleague? How did the conversation help you make decisions and develop solutions that were effective? What was the outcome?

- How often do you make brief, unannounced visits to classrooms? What is the purpose of your visits? Has the time spent in classrooms improved the quality of teaching? Why or why not?

Action Tool

- Think about your own skill set for engaging in professional conversations. Complete the Listening Skills Inventory provided in Figure 5.1. Reflect on your personal strengths and areas for growth as an instructional leader. Identify steps can you take to strengthen future conversations with teachers.

• Using the Topics for Conversation and Guiding Questions in Table 5.1, conduct three, informal classroom visits each week for a period of three weeks. Follow up each visit with a conversation with the teacher, using the protocol presented in this chapter. Record your visits and reflections on the table provided in Table 5.2.

Figure 5.1   Listening Skills Inventory

	Almost Always	Sometimes	Seldom	Don't Know/ Unaware
1. My purpose for talking with teachers is transparent.				
2. I ask questions with positive intentions and a presumption of competence, not criticism.				
3. I comment about teachers' *islands of competence* during a conversation.				
4. I know the teacher's *just right* level.				
5. I ask questions at the teacher's *just right* level that help extend their thinking and develop their own ideas.				
6. I refrain from making a judgment about the speaker before hearing what he or she has to say.				
7. I refrain from solution listening.				
8. I refrain from autobiographical listening.				
9. I refrain from inquisitive listening.				
10. I provide with constructive, specific feedback to the teacher.				
11. I consider the assumptions embedded in the questions I ask.				
12. When I am listening, I make a conscious effort to periodically make eye contact with the speaker.				
13. I make an effort to minimize outside distractions when I am talking with a teacher.				
14. I frequently pause or am silent when waiting for a teacher's response.				
15. I paraphrase what I have heard to clarify understanding.				
16. I ask questions to clarify statements that I may not fully understand.				
17. I listen more than I talk.				
18. I seek feedback from teachers to help improve the quality of our conversations.				

Table 5.2 Classroom Visit Log

Date of Visit	Time (Start–End)	Teacher	Tenured	Non-Tenured	Date of Follow-up Conversation
Week 1					
Week 2					
Week 3					

Reflections and Ideas for Next Steps

Use the space below to summarize your experiences. What went well? What surprised you? How did the teachers respond? What did you learn? What will you do next?

_____

_____

_____

_____

_____

_____

_____

_____

6

Principals Can't Lead Alone

The Role of the District Office

District offices have been a largely ignored resource for schools as they seek to improve teaching and learning.

Kaufman, Grimm, and Miller (2012)

Improving Instruction: Does the Central Office Matter?

The role of the superintendent and the district office is well documented in the professional literature yet still remains a mystery to most people in or outside of education. One might ask, who are the people who hold these positions, and what do they have to do with teaching and learning? Are these positions really necessary? Many teachers will say they've had few conversations with central office staff. Aside from a few annual district functions like the opening day of school, year-end awards assemblies, or state championship games, many central office staff are rarely seen out and about, interacting with teachers and students. And yet, the participation of central office administrators is essential to improving the quality of teaching and learning. This chapter examines the critical role of district office personnel in providing the resources needed to build strong, instructional leaders who are capable of improving teacher quality and student learning across a district.

A Case in Point

The work of former Superintendent Anthony Alvarado of New York City Community School District #2 was documented in a case study authored by Richard Elmore and Deanna Burney (1997). This case illustrates the influence a district office can have in building capacity, establishing accountability, and nurturing innovation. Under Superintendent Alvarado, Community School District #2 leaders developed a vision for improvement that focused on a system-wide improvement through the use of research-based instructional practices, professional development to effectively implement these practices, instructional leadership, and a high level of accountability. Alvarado's successes were studied and replicated by other superintendents and central offices because these efforts resulted in sustained improvements in teaching and student learning.

Marzano and Waters (2009) found that "there is a .24 correlation between district leadership and student achievement and a .25 correlation between school leadership and student achievement" (p. 87), which illustrates the importance of strong district-wide leadership in improving student performance and achievement. Sparks (2002) argues that it is imperative for districts to articulate expectations for student learning, teaching, leadership, and professional development followed up with accountability and incentives for reaching these expectations. Elmore (2000) believes that districts that have sustained improvements in student learning have superintendents who possess a strong knowledge base about teaching and learning. This was certainly the case with Anthony Alvarado who initiated capacity building initiatives that led to improvement in learning and professional practice.

Increased Accountability for Leaders

Increased accountability for all students has been the impetus for district leaders to pay more attention to student data and take necessary actions to ensure improved student outcomes. As a result, principals today are more responsible for continuous and sustainable improvements in teaching and learning than ever before. This has led to the adoption of more rigorous performance evaluations for principals and teachers associated with President Barak Obama's educational reform agenda, Race to the Top.

Prior to the adoption of the federal No Child Left Behind act (NCLB), principals were evaluated based upon how effectively they managed and operated their buildings, handled student discipline, and pleased their staff and community. NCLB changed the rules of the game with its focus on closing the achievement gap and holding states, districts, and schools—thereby principals—accountable for student performance across all student groups.

Today, words such as value-added and student growth models have become the norm in legislation across the country in discussions about how to ensure that all students are meeting higher, more rigorous standards for learning and achievement. These terms have also been discussed quite a bit in teachers' lunch rooms and at union meetings around the country. Under Race to the Top, teacher performance is based on teaching performance as well as student achievement and growth. Principal performance is also based on student achievement and evidence of instructional leadership. These rigorous requirements have changed the expectations for the way principals spend their time during the instructional day. While the label "instructional leader" has been around for some time, this model for leadership does not emerge unless it is an explicit and deliberate goal of a school district with the influence of the school system's model instructional leader, the superintendent.

The following case study is based on actual events that took place in a large suburban school district. It demonstrates the impact a superintendent and district office team have when they focus on professional development for *every adult learner in the system.*

Creating a Culture for Professional Learning: A Case Study

A Powerful First Impression

Magna Romano's experience provides an example of how a superintendent can influence teacher learning—right from the start. Magna attended a new teacher job fair held in a former armory in a large urban school district. She dressed in the new suit she bought for interviews and brought multiple copies of her resume. When she arrived, Magna looked around to assess her competition. Dressed for success, everyone had a look of confidence and determination that this was going to be the day that they were hired for their first teaching position. As Magna scoped out the room, she noticed a superintendent from one of the districts where she was interested in teaching, and he was walking around greeting prospective candidates. It was no surprise to Magna that teacher candidates were lining up for a five minute interview with this district. The district had a reputation for innovative practices in literacy and an extensive support system for new teachers. When Magna got her turn to speak with the superintendent, he asked her to share her views about teaching and learning. What did an effective literacy program look like? How would she use cooperative learning to increase student engagement? How would she differentiate instruction to increase student learning? Magna was impressed with his selection of questions, all of them relating to important topics of teaching and learning. As a result of this screening interview, Magna was offered her first teaching position right on the spot.

At the opening day convocation, the superintendent began his speech to the staff by celebrating the districts' successes from the previous year and presented the charge for the coming year, which was to ensure that teachers used research-based practices to improve the outcomes for all learners. The message that stuck with Magna was that "individuals can't be what the organization that they are in is not." The superintendent emphasized that schools and school districts, like other organizations, shape individuals, and individuals shape the organizations that they inhabit. His plan to shape the school district included an increased focus on professional development for instructional and noninstructional staff. He also pledged additional time for teams of teachers to collaborate in an effort to improve reading and writing skills of all students by providing an authentic context using technology as a tool. He told the audience of both instructional and noninstructional staff members that they could expect to see him in their schools and classrooms throughout the year. He wanted to witness firsthand the implementation of these initiatives and support both principals and teachers in achieving these goals. When the convocation ended, Magna watched the superintendent shaking hands with staff members as they exited, thanking them for their contributions to the district. Magna left the convocation with enthusiasm about her new position, excited that she would have an opportunity to work with and learn from others to achieve the goals articulated by the superintendent.

Months and years later, Magna lost count of the number of times that she saw the superintendent in her school and her own classroom.

It was not uncommon to see him kneeling next to a student to ask what they were learning and why this was important to learn. She remembered that he always would ask students if he could read their written work or if they could read to him. It was not uncommon for him to enter the classroom and be greeted by several students who asked him to read their work. Because he was actively engaged when he visited classrooms and visible throughout the district, he didn't need to depend upon others to tell him what was happening in classrooms and schools.

Magna's experience illustrates the role that the superintendent plays in shaping the culture of a district around what matters most—improving learning for all students. The superintendent established district-wide goals that were the focus for every school and frequently visited classrooms and schools to see evidence of the implementation of these goals.

Magna Romano's career path eventually led her to become a building level leader. After several years in this position, she was promoted to assistant superintendent of instruction, curriculum, and professional development in a large suburban district. It became clear to Magna in a relatively short period of time that the purpose of the central office was to improve teaching and learning. This was the vision developed by her newly hired superintendent, Dr. Martha Cullen. Dr. Cullen defined the mission of the central office as a place to build capacity for ongoing improvement in teaching and learning and to create the conditions that fostered student success. The board of education selected Dr. Cullen to lead the team as the new superintendent of Esterfield Unified School District with a charge to build on the past success of the district while ensuring that schools were provided with the resources they needed to increase learning outcomes for all students. They wanted Dr. Cullen to ensure that even the high performing schools would not be standing still when it came to making the system even better.

A History of Principal Autonomy

When Dr. Cullen arrived, the district had a history of giving principals a great deal of autonomy in how they ran their schools. Each school building in Esterfield was unique, which meant that principals operated their building around a set of priorities that were important to students, teachers, and parents in their school. Building principals selected their own resources, hired excellent teachers, and subscribed to a belief that positive student outcomes meant that teachers were effectively meeting the needs of all learners. The former superintendent had a reputation for keeping a close watch on student achievement while encouraging autonomy among principals.

When Dr. Cullen first met with building principals, it was clear that they were proud of their staff and students. When asked about professional development opportunities for teachers, most principals agreed this was not a priority of the district. With student outcomes remaining stable over the past ten years, teacher learning was not seen as a necessity. With the exception of a few conferences attended by teachers in specialized programs, professional development was reserved for newly hired professionals. Superintendent's conference days, traditionally devoted to professional learning, were dedicated to parent–teacher conferences and meetings around grade level or team level goals. The principals had complete discretion in planning and organizing these days.

Despite a lack of focus on professional learning, the district remained a top performing district in the region with 97 percent of the students graduating and attending two and four year colleges. As the new superintendent, Dr. Cullen's goal was to celebrate and build upon the success of her predecessor and develop an entry plan supported by the board of education that would focus on initiatives that would move the district from being "good to great" (Collins, 2001). Dr. Cullen recognized that the most important role of a superintendent is improving student learning. To be successful in this work, she knew she needed to build a central office leadership team that would implement and monitor the district's priorities and goals. Now was the time to get the team together.

Getting the Right Members on the Team

Selection of members of the central office leadership team is comparable to a manager who recruits and drafts team members for a professional athletic franchise. The manager knows that he has to meticulously and strategically select athletes who are not only talented at what they do, but are able to work in sync toward a common goal. The superintendent has to select team members whose expertise and talents can be collectively leveraged to carry out a vision and set goals for improving student learning.

Dr. Cullen set out to create a central office team that had a strong knowledge base about research-based practices, professional learning communities, and professional development. When she was appointed, she had unanimous support from the board of education to make a number of strategic changes at the central office that immediately established her priorities as the system's instructional leader. The implementation of these changes sent a powerful message throughout the district that improving student achievement and instruction were non-negotiable.

In his book *Shaking up the Schoolhouse,* Schlechty (2001) maintains that "school system leaders, particularly superintendents, must acquire certain skills, concepts, and understandings . . . so their leadership initiates and sustains change-adept schools and school districts that will achieve uncommon results for all or nearly all students" (p. 187). He identified a number of key competencies essential for superintendents which include marketing the need for change, building a sense of community, forging compelling beliefs and communicating vision, organizing all district and school activity around the work of students, using assessment and managing results, fostering innovation and continuous improvement, fostering collaboration, and investing in professional development.

Dr. Cullen made sure that she selected members of the team who embodied these competencies. She restructured the positions of the director of elementary education and the director of secondary education to create two cabinet level positions: Office of Student Learning and Office of Instruction and Professional Development. These new positions embodied the priorities of the district of improving student learning and teacher practice. The superintendent created a budget code for professional development under the new Office of Instruction and Professional Development to establish resources for job embedded professional learning for all instructional and noninstructional employee groups. In addition, the Office of Student Learning created a venue for ongoing professional learning by dedicating two hours a month to professional development for central office administrators, principals, and department chairs. As a result of this change, monthly leadership team meetings were spent reading and discussing professional literature related to ways the instructional leader could support student learning and achievement.

Over the next five years, principals, assistant principals, department chairs, and teacher leaders amassed a professional library of research on best practice. The expectation was that the library would be shared and disseminated to school faculty and departments to encourage ongoing, collaborative inquiry about student learning and professional practice. District leaders were expected to ensure that all roads led to improved student learning, achievement, and enhanced professional practice. For this work to be accomplished, central office leadership would need to develop a structure for professional development that was job embedded, collaborative, and sustainable by each school. The work began at the top, led by the superintendent and central office leadership team.

Learning for All Adults in the System

The superintendent and the central office leadership team laid the foundation for system-wide improvements using professional development as the key strategy for change. These improvements began with bimonthly superintendent's cabinet meetings that included directors and assistant superintendents focused on improving student learning and strengthening professional practice as the primary goal of an instructional leader second only to the health, safety, and well-being of children and the staff. It was important for members of the team, even the business officials, to be reminded of how their role impacted teaching and learning.

Dr. Cullen knew that what was talked about the most became the focus in the district and was thus accomplished. The team read and shared the book *Know Can Do: Put Your Know-How Into Action* (Blanchard, Meyer, & Ruhe, 2007), which examines the gap between knowledge and implementation (*knowing* and *doing*). Blanchard identified a lack of follow-up or repetition and negative thinking as key culprits in thwarting and derailing change initiatives. Reading and discussing the message of this book reinforced the team's thinking about the importance of staying focused on the goals and priorities of the system and communicating a hopeful, "can do" message as a model for other leaders to follow.

Aligning School and District Goals and Priorities

The message from central office was clear: professional development was for every adult learner in the system. The superintendent needed to ensure that principals were able to identify researched-based instructional models that would result in improved student outcomes. Aside from managing their buildings, principals had to be able to use their student achievement data to identify what would make the greatest impact on student learning.

At the start of the school year, the principals met with the assistant superintendent of student learning to set targets for improvements based on an analysis of the available student data. The improvement targets submitted by the principals included increasing student mastery of specific performance indicators in English and mathematics, increasing the performance of students with disabilities on state assessments, reducing the number of students who needed academic intervention services, creating more Tier II or III interventions for Response to Intervention, and developing ways to decrease incidents of student bullying. Each principal submitted their school action plan to the central office where the plans were carefully reviewed by central office leaders to ensure that they reflected the district's priority goals, which had been established through a strategic planning process.

The district's priority goals provided a broad focus on how the school system would improve student achievement and teacher practice. They served as a template for all functions of the district including budget planning, professional development, resource allocation and recruitment, and staffing. To ensure there was ongoing accountability for the stated goals and targets, the principals needed to demonstrate that students were responding to the supports and interventions put in place to promote greater success. To accomplish this, the principals accompanied the superintendent and assistant superintendent in classroom walk-throughs and met once a month with the superintendent and a member of her central office team to discuss the following guiding questions:

- Which students are performing below the standards, and what are the root causes?
- Discuss six to eight data points being used to monitor student progress including pre- and post-tests.
- What instructional practices, strategies, interventions and resources are being used to ensure improvement in student learning and progress of individual learners?
- What will you do differently if students do not reach the established goals?
- What are you doing to ensure that students who are meeting the standards maintain or exceed these goals?

These conversations were invaluable because they established the connection between professional learning and student learning. This process helped the superintendent and her leadership team to identify principals who were experiencing success and those who needed additional assistance or coaching. Engaging in ongoing meetings with principals to review learning data further strengthened Dr. Cullen's belief that what was focused on was implemented.

Teacher Evaluation a Tool for Teacher Learning

Dr. Cullen understood that improving opportunities for students required teachers to engage in professional growth. She believed that an effective teacher evaluation process could promote professional learning, provided that instructional leaders were equipped with the right understandings and skills. The decision to adopt Charlotte Danielson's seminal work *Enhancing Professional Practice: A Framework for Teaching* (2009) as the basis for teacher evaluation in the district laid the foundation for principals and central office leaders to develop a common language about instruction and learning. The Framework for Teaching became the blueprint for effective practice across the district. Leaders from the district and building levels, along with teachers, selected the Framework because it focused on the conditions needed for students to learn rather than on what teachers did or didn't do. This was a complete departure from the subjective process used prior to the adoption of the Danielson model.

A key decision the central office made was to engage a consultant to help facilitate this process, someone who was a colleague of Danielson, with a deep understanding of her work. The central office leadership team worked with the consultant to develop a plan that would ensure all professional staff members would learn about the Framework as a tool to improve teaching and learning. A group of administrators and teacher leaders worked with the consultant over several months, learning to lead activities around the Framework with teachers in their own buildings.

The district understood that to build consistency and reliability into the new evaluation system, leaders from all levels would need training, practice, and spaced repetition. Alongside the central office team leaders, the consultant accompanied teams of principals, assistant principals, and department chairs into classrooms to collect evidence of teaching, then compared and discussed the evidence they collected. To ensure continued growth and learning, she recommended key resources that the central office leadership team procured for principals and teachers ranging from a resource on strategies that fostered student engagement to tools that helped teachers ask higher level questions.

The consultant periodically met with the principals and central office leaders, including the superintendent, over the next five years to help them to internalize the use of the framework for teaching and sustain the focus on using the evaluation system to improve teaching and learning. Overtime, Dr. Cullen began to see evidence that the evaluation system was also a tool for improving *student* learning. When she visited classrooms, she saw more student collaboration and the use of technology where students created blogs on books and articles that they were reading or Skype sessions with editors of magazines or newspapers. She observed students sharing their opinions and backing them up with evidence from texts that they were using.

She witnessed an increase in critical thinking and problem solving at all levels of learning. Dr. Cullen noticed that across the system, more so than ever, the central office administrative team and principals were using the same language to describe what constituted good teaching and agreed upon what caused active student engagement.

Esterfield Unified School District had successfully built a structure for ongoing, job embedded learning for district and school leaders. They used monthly meetings to learn and discuss best practice, they had a system for tracking building level targets and providing support when it was indicated, and they learned how to make teacher evaluation an opportunity for teacher learning. Now it was time to feed the teachers.

Professional Development as the Fuel for the System

Another key decision the superintendent made was to engage the assistant superintendent for instruction and professional development in the task of establishing building-based professional development teams. Every principal was asked to identify teacher leaders from across their faculty and assemble a building-based professional development team that would ultimately direct the type of professional learning that would occur at their building. This was uncharted territory for the school system. Prior to the arrival of the new superintendent, there was no link made between student achievement and professional learning.

Some principals and teachers took offense to the notion that they needed to continue to grow and learn as professionals. It was not uncommon for Dr. Cullen to be reminded by a principal, board member, teacher, or parent that Esterfield was a high performing district; they didn't need any professional development. In their minds, professional development was only for districts that were in trouble. Previous professional development experiences where they sat and listened (for hours) to an outside expert left them cynical and convinced that professional development was a waste of time and money. They did not subscribe to the belief that you don't have to be bad to get better and "organizations that stand still do not move forward" (Robbins & Alvy, 2004, p. 59). Members of the district were not shy about sharing their opinions.

The superintendent was determined to reverse this attitude toward professional learning held by most in the system. She set out to create a model for professional development that would lead to principal and teacher buy-in and participation. The assistant superintendent visited each principal to describe the roles and responsibilities of the school-based professional development team and the criteria for selecting teachers and specialists to serve on the team. The principals were excited that they and their staff would have a role in designing their building-based professional development plan, which would be aligned to the district's plan. Principals needed to select staff members from across grade, content, and support specialists and recruit those who had influence among the staff and who could be positive messengers of this change. The principals could select as many members to serve on the building-based professional development team as needed.

Once these building level teams were established, they participated in after school and summer professional development workshops to learn how to collaborate, function effectively as a team, and establish norms that would help them to achieve their goals around improving student learning and professional practice. The central office leadership team decided to negotiate an incentive with the teachers' union for members who participated in professional development that took place after school or during the summer. While the rate of forty dollars an hour insulted some, others were grateful that they received compensation for their time.

The establishment of norms of practice for engagement in ongoing, collaborative inquiry gained further support through the implementation of the Inquiry Team model, a provision of the Race to the Top reform agenda in New York State. This team of teachers and specialists under the leadership of the school principal demonstrated the importance of several characteristics of high performing districts that Reeves (2006) believes are critical for sustaining high achievement for all students. These include holistic accountability, early interventions, rigorous curriculum, common assessments, and an understanding of how to use data to improve student learning. All of these essential ingredients became a part of the "new" work of schools under the watchful eye of the new superintendent and her team.

Expanding Professional Learning Across the District

To fuel the learning of the building level teams, a district-wide professional development team was created, which was populated by several representatives from each building-based team. Once a month after school, this team came together to explore job embedded practices such as study groups, walk-throughs, lesson study, video dialogues, critical friends groups, data analysis, and protocols for examining student work. They took these practices back to their building-based teams to introduce during faculty meetings, grade level and department meetings, early release professional development days, and superintendent's conference days. These protocols served to guide the work of the building teams, focusing on what mattered most in improving learning and teaching.

In addition, throughout the school year, workshops were offered after school and over the summer to introduce staff to these job embedded protocols that could help them solve problems around learning and practice. The workshops were added to the district professional development site so that anyone in the school system could access and use them. During scheduled conference and early release days, school-based professional development teams offered their own workshops on these protocols for their colleagues. As an additional measure of support, the assistant superintendent created slides and supporting materials that could be used as is or retooled by the building team, a valuable time saving resource. The access to these resources also facilitated the likelihood that these job embedded protocols would be used across the district.

According to Elmore (2003) "the selection a school makes regarding its work (that is what to work on next) is perhaps the most critical factor in the school's ability to improve student achievement" (p. 90). The superintendent and central office leadership team focused a great deal of attention on providing resources to replicate and disseminate good practices. They needed to know if the work of the building-based professional development teams was having an impact at the classroom level. An important resource created for this purpose was a DVD that modeled how to conduct a brief classroom visit. Created by the assistant superintendent and her team, the purpose was to build skills and provide practice for principals and teachers to engage in collaborative classroom visits. These visits would provide a way for the district and building team to know if the practices led by the building level teams were being embedded in the core of instruction.

The process was outlined at a monthly professional development team meeting and the DVD was linked to the professional development site in Google. The use of Google supported the notion of anytime and anywhere learning. Principals and teachers were encouraged to sign up to participate in a group learning walk or host one in their building. Central office leaders also signed up to participate. Teachers were informed that the purpose of the classroom visits was to collect data on the presence of practices that were in place that would impact student learning. The data collected would be shared with the building-based professional development team. This process developed a cycle of continuous improvement.

The principals expressed concerns about finding time to try out the job embedded protocols that they had learned to use. Although time is a resource all educators struggle with, the superintendent entertained ideas from the principals and her team about how to create more time for professional learning that wouldn't result in the loss of instructional time.

Finding Time for Professional Learning

From the beginning of Dr. Cullen's appointment as superintendent, the central office leadership team had numerous discussions with the teachers' and principals' union about the timing of professional development during the school year. The greatest challenge was how to minimize loss of instructional time for students. The superintendent and her central office team did not want teachers pulled out of the classroom. Based on feedback from teachers and principals, they devised a solution to add additional half days to the school calendar. This option meant that three times a year, students would be released several hours before the regular dismissal schedule to allow principals and their school staff to participate in professional development created by their building level team. The building team agendas were submitted to the professional development site in Google several weeks before the conference or early release day so that the superintendent and central office leadership could review their goals and outcomes.

In addition, on conference and early release days, the central office leadership team was assigned to visit schools to join a professional learning session. Their observations and experiences were shared at the next superintendent's staff meeting. Feedback was provided to the principals to celebrate their successes or suggest improvements. Teachers and principals acknowledged that this approach to establishing the agenda around their needs for professional development led to meaningful and relevant professional learning.

Securing the Future of Leaders and the Professional Staff

Dr. Cullen and her leadership team left nothing to chance when it came to supporting the needs of new leaders and teachers. A number of long serving principals had retired and been replaced with promising new principals who were in their first role as principal. Some of the principals were welcomed by volatile school communities where parents and teachers wanted the new leader to hit the ground running.

To support the new principals a New Leaders Institute was created to surround them with a support system that would help them succeed as leaders. The New Leaders Institute was held for two days in July. New central office administrators also attended the institute. The goal of the institute was to help the new leaders gain an understanding of the district's expectations for them as instructional leaders. A sample New Leaders Institute agenda is provided in Figure 6.1.

During the institute, they discussed instruction, curriculum, and professional development initiatives that were underway in the district. In addition, they practiced using the tools of the teacher evaluation system, learned about budget and purchasing procedures, and learned about the student and data management systems. Each new leader received a mentor selected by the central office leadership team who attended the New Leaders Institute with the new leader.

The district also recognized that new *and experienced* principals could benefit from working with a leadership coach who would help them work on aspects of instructional leadership that they needed to improve. The introduction of a leadership coach was an acknowledgement that principals, similar to teachers, fell along a developmental continuum based on their longevity, experience, and expertise. Principals were placed in teams of three or four and met with the leadership coach three times a year. The teams of principals collaborated on the creation of the agenda that would be sent to the coach prior to the meeting. This gave the coach an opportunity to prepare resources to support the principals. The coach also met with the superintendent and her team to discuss concerns or share suggestions that emerged from conversations with the principals.

Each summer, probationary teachers and professional staff would attend a New Professionals Institute that was a requirement for all tenure track staff members. When Dr. Cullen arrived, two key changes were made that strengthened the institute. First, the name was changed from the New Teacher Institute to the New Professionals Institute which acknowledged that school counselors, library media specialists, psychologists, and speech and language specialists were essential members of the school support team. The other key change was to streamline the agenda and narrow the topics of the institute to increase the focus on improving student outcomes. The new agenda was organized around the four domains of Danielson's Framework. During the summer institute, the new professionals examined teaching and student learning by observing lessons and collecting evidence on several of the domains and components that they would be observed on in their first, second, and third years as probationary staff. Over time, the probationary staff members became experienced in using the

Framework and as a result, became the "go to" people who were often called upon to assist more senior professional staff members.

Many of these new professionals became members of the building-based professional development teams and led workshops on conference and early release days for their experienced colleagues. The New Professionals Institute contributes to building a district-wide culture around effective instructional practice and a common understanding about teaching that makes the greatest impact on student learning.

Key Points About the Role of the District Office

The story of Magna Romano, Dr. Martha Cullen, and her central office staff in the Esterfield Unified School district paints a vivid picture of how the district office matters. The superintendent shapes and communicates a vision around improved student outcomes. Members of the central office leadership team carry out this vision by supporting principals in transforming the vision into positive changes that can be seen in classrooms.

All of the adults in a school district need to grow, learn, and work together on behalf of children. The reforms starting with NCLB and the newest member of the reform family, Race to the Top, demand the collective attention, talents, and skills of all stakeholders to ensure that new curriculum and the next generation of assessments are implemented and improve student learning. By teaming with school leaders to develop goals that are aligned with district goals and priorities, providing varied models of professional development that are built from the bottom up, and monitoring the progress of goals through careful oversight, the district office has the potential to dramatically influence the quality of teaching and learning.

Putting Words Into Action

Action Tool

The Instructional Leadership Inventory (Figure 6.1) is a tool that may be used by the superintendent and members of the central office leadership team to assess how their current role and responsibilities place them in contact with schools, principals, and teachers around instruction and learning. By conducting this inventory, the superintendent and the central office leadership team will be able to identify specific goals to increase opportunities that directly improve the outcomes for all learners.

Ninety minutes should be set aside to respond to the inventory items, discuss the follow up questions, and develop an action plan. The inventory may also be completed prior to meeting as a team.

Figure 6.1   Instructional Leadership Inventory

	Always	Sometimes	Never
I spend time daily speaking to others about improving instruction and learning.			
I spend time in classrooms observing instruction and learning.			
When I visit classrooms, I interact with students by asking them questions about what they are learning or by reviewing their written work.			
I provide feedback to principals about their progress in meeting their goals for improving instruction and learning.			
I am formally assigned to observe instructional staff every year.			
I participate in professional learning with principals who are implementing new instructional practices.			
I use instructional rounds or learning walks to monitor the progress that principals are making toward improving student learning.			
I participate in district-wide or school-based data inquiry teams to review student progress on specific strategies and skills.			
I recommend research-based instructional practices and resources to principals and teachers that will improve student learning.			
I follow up and monitor the progress of the research-based instructional practices and resources that I recommend.			
I attend workshops with teachers who are learning new instructional practices.			
I participate in the analysis of student work samples and discussions and to monitor student learning.			
I attend local or national professional conferences that focus on instruction and learning and bring back and implement what I've learned.			
I participate in book discussions or study groups with my colleagues or others to expand my knowledge base about what constitutes effective instructional practices or what will improve student learning.			
The superintendent and the central office leadership team spend time during cabinet meetings discussing how to improve instruction and learning.			

Reflect and Assess

- What surprised you about your responses to the inventory?
- What can you do to improve the percentage of time that you spend devoted to these instructional improvement activities?
- What can the team can do make the greatest impact on student learning?

REFERENCES

Appleton, J. J., Christenson, S. L., & Furlong, J. J. (2008). Student engagement with school: Critical conceptual and methodological issues of the construct. *Psychology in Schools, 45*(5), 369–386.

Beteille, T., Kalogrides, D., & Loeb, S. (2011). Stepping stones: Principal career path and school outcomes. *Social Science Research, 41*(4), 909–919.

Blanchard, K., Meyer, P. J., & Ruhe, D. (2007). *Know can do! Putting your know-how into action.* San Francisco, CA: Berrett-Koehler.

Bryk, A. S., & Schneider, B. (2003). Trust in schools: A core resource for school reform. *Educational Leadership, 60*(6), 40–45.

Cheliotes, L. G., & Reilly, M. F. (2010). *Coaching conversations: Transforming your school one conversation at a time.* Thousand Oaks, CA: Corwin.

City, E. A., Elmore, R. F., Fiarman, S. E., & Teitel, L. (2009). *Instructional rounds in education.* Cambridge, MA: Harvard Education Press.

Collins, J. (2001). *Good to great: Why some companies make the leap . . . and others don't.* New York, NY: Harper Collins.

Connors, N. A. (2000). *If you don't feed the teachers they eat the students!* Nashville, TN: Incentive Publications.

Conzemius, A., & O'Neill, J. (2001). *Building shared responsibility for student learning.* Alexandria, VA: Association for Supervision and Curriculum Development.

Croft, A., Coggshall, J. G., Dolan, M., Powers, E., & Killion, J. (2010). *Job-embedded professional development: What it is, who is responsible, and how to get it done well.* (Issue Brief April 2010). Washington, DC: National Comprehensive Center for Teacher Quality.

Danielson, C. (2007). *Enhancing professional practice: A framework for teaching* (2nd ed.). Alexandria, VA: Association for Supervision and Curriculum Development.

Danielson, C. (2009). *Talk about teaching!* Thousand Oaks, CA: Corwin.

Danielson, C., Axtell, D., Bevan, P., Cleland, B., McKay, C., Phillips, E., & Wright, K. (2009). *Implementing the framework for teaching in enhancing professional practice.* Alexandria, VA: Association for Supervision and Curriculum and Development.

Davenport, T. H. (2005). *Thinking for a living: How to get better performance and results from knowledge workers.* Boston, MA: Harvard Business Press.

Deal, T., & Peterson, K. (2009). *Shaping school culture* (2nd ed.). San Francisco, CA: Jossey-Bass.

Donaldson, M. L. (2009). *So long, Lake Wobegon? Using teacher evaluation to raise teacher quality*. Washington, DC: Center for American Progress.

Downey, C. J., Steffy, B. E., Fenwick, W. E., Frase, L. E., & Poston, W. K. (2004). *The three-minute classroom walkthrough: Changing supervisory practice one teacher at a time*. Thousand Oaks, CA: Corwin.

DuFour, R. (2003). "Collaboration lite" puts student achievement on a starvation diet. *Journal of Staff Development, 24*(3), 63–64.

Dweck, C. S. (2006). *Mindset*. New York, NY: Random House.

Elmore, R. F. (2000). *Building a new structure for school leadership*. Washington, DC: The Albert Shanker Institute.

Elmore, R. F. (2003). *Knowing the right thing to do: School improvement and performance-based accountability*. Washington, DC: NGA Center for Best Practices.

Elmore, R. F. (2010). "I used to think . . . and now I think . . . " *Harvard Education Letter, 26*(1), 1–3.

Elmore, R., & Burney, D. (1997). *Investing in teacher learning: Staff development and instructional improvement in Community School District # 2, New York City*. New York, NY: Consortium for Policy Research in Education (CPRE).

Evans, R. (1996). *The human side of change*. San Francisco, CA: Jossey-Bass.

Fink, E., & Resnick, L. B. (2001). Developing principals as instructional leaders. *Phi Delta Kappan, 82*(8), 598.

Fullan, M. (2003). *The moral imperative of school leadership*. Thousand Oaks, CA: Corwin.

Fuller E., & Young, M. D. (2009, Summer). *Tenure and retention of newly hired principals in Texas* (Issue Brief No. 1). Austin, TX: Texas High School Project Leadership Initiative.

Guskey, T. (1999). *Evaluating professional development*. Thousand Oaks, CA: Corwin.

Horng, E. L., Klasik, D., & Loeb, S. (2009) *Principal time-use and school effectiveness*. Stanford, CA: Institute for Research on Education Policy & Practice.

Ing, M. (2010). Using informal classroom observations to improve instruction. *Journal of Educational Administration, 48*(3), 337–358.

Kauffman, T. E., Grimm, E. D., & Miller, A. (2012). School and district collaboration: The secret to scaling up school reform. *Education Week, 31*(28), 25.

Knight, J. (2009). What can we do about teacher resistance? *Phi Delta Kappan, 90*(7), 508–513.

Leithwood, K., Louis, K. S., Anderson, S., & Wahlstrom, K. (2004). *How leadership influences student learning*. The Wallace Foundation.

Marlowe, B. A., & Page, M. L. (2000). Battered teacher syndrome. *Education Week, 20*(15), 43–46.

Marlowe, B. A., & Page, M. L. (2005). *Creating and sustaining the constructivist classroom* (2nd ed.). Thousand Oaks, CA: Corwin.

Martin-Kniep, G., & Picone-Zocchia, J. (2009). *Changing the way you teach: Improving the way students learn*. Alexandria, VA: Association for Supervision and Curriculum Development.

Marzano, R. J., & Water, T. (2009). *District leadership that works: Striking the right balance.* Bloomington, IN: Solution Tree Press.

New Teacher Project. (2010). *Teacher evaluation 2.0.* Brooklyn, NY: Author.

Reeves, D. B. (2009). *Leading change in your school.* Washington, DC: Association for Supervision and Curriculum Development.

Reeves, D. B. (2006). *The learning leader: How to focus school improvement for better results.* Alexandria, VA: Association for Supervision and Curriculum Development.

Reeves, D. B. (2007). Leading to change/closing the implementation gap. *Educational Leadership, 64*(6), 85–86.

Robbins, P., & Alvy, H. (2004). *The new principal's fieldbook: Strategies for success.* Alexandria, VA: Association for Supervision and Curriculum Development.

Rose-colored glasses. (2012). Dictionary.infoplease.com. Pearson Education. Retrieved from http://www.dictionary.infoplease.com/rose-colored-glasses

Schlechty, P. C. (2001). *Shaking up the schoolhouse.* San Francisco, CA: Jossey-Bass.

Schmoker, M. (2006). *Results now.* Washington, DC: Association for Supervision and Curriculum Development.

Sergiovanni, T. J. (2005). The virtues of leadership. *The Educational Forum,* 69, Winter 2005, 112.

Shulman, L. S. (2004). *The wisdom of practice: Essays on teaching, learning, and learning to teach.* San Francisco, CA: Jossey-Bass.

Sousa, D. A. (2009). Brain-Friendly learning for teachers. *Educational Leadership Online,* 66. Retrieved from http://www.ascd.org/publications/educational_leadership/summer09/vol66/num09/Brain-Friendly_Learning_For_Teachers.aspx

Sousa, D. A. (2011). *How the brain learns* (4th ed.). Thousand Oaks, CA: Corwin.

Sparks, D. (2002). *Designing powerful professional development for teachers and principals.* Oxford, OH: National Staff Development Council.

Strong, R. W., Silver, H. F., & Perini, M. J. (2001). *Teaching what matters most.* Alexandria, VA: Association for Supervision and Curriculum Development.

Tharp, R. G., Estrada, P., Dalton, S. S., & Yamauchi, L. A. (2000). *Teaching transformed: Achieving excellence, fairness, inclusion, and harmony.* Boulder, CO: Westview Press.

Walser, N. (2011). The virtues of experience. *Harvard Education Letter, 27*(1), 6–8.

Weisberg, D., Sexton, S., Mulhern, J. & Keeling, D. (2009). *The widget effect: Our national failure to acknowledge and act on differences in teacher effectiveness.* Brooklyn, NY: The New Teacher Project.

Whitaker, T. (2003). *What great principals do differently: Fifteen things that matter most.* Larchmont, NY: Eye on Education.

Williams, J S. (2003). Why great teachers stay. *Educational Leadership, 60*(8), 71–74.

Index

Albert Shanker Institute, 8
American Educational Research Journal, 37
Autobiographical listening, 56-57

"Battered Teacher Syndrome" (Marlowe and Page), 69-70
Belief statements, 30-31, 34*f*
Blanchard, K., 112
"Brain-Friendly Learning for Teachers" (Sousa), 57-58
Building Shared Responsibility for Student Learning (Conzemius and O'Neill), 28

Capturing School History, 37-38*f*
Center for American Progress, 20
Central Regional School District, 3-6
Cheliotes, L., 86
Classroom observation, 52-54
Classroom visit:
    constructive feedback, 96, 99
    conversation opportunity, 95-96
    conversation protocol, 97, 99-101
    conversation topics, 96-97, 98*t*, 103
    culture of learning development, 24-26
    district office role, 113
    formal observation, 95
    guiding questions, 96, 98*t*
    informal observation, 95-96
    postobservation conference, 89, 97, 99, 100-101
    principal experience, 88-89
    professional conversations, 87-88, 95-97, 98*t*, 99-101, 103
    purpose clarification, 87-89

Classroom Visit Log, 104*f*
Coaching, 54-55
Coaching Conversations (Cheliotes and Reilly), 86
Commitment statements, 31-32, 34*f*
Connors, N., 71
Constructive feedback:
    instructional leadership skills, 57-58
    professional conversations, 96, 99
Conzemius, A., 28
Courage, L., 84-85
Criticism, 56
Cullen, M., 109-120
Culture of learning development:
    action tools, 37-38
    belief statements, 30-31, 34*f*
    classroom visits, 24-26
    commitment statements, 31-32, 34*f*
    continuous improvement cycle, 26-27
    culture of nice, 19-21
    educational reform, 21-22
    Historygram process, 28-30, 37-38*f*
    key points, 35-36
    knowledge workers, 26-27
    Lake Wobegon effect, 21
    leadership actions, 32-35
    leadership role, 22-28
    learning opportunities, 34-35
    professional journals, 37
    reflection questions, 36-37
    spaced-repetition technique, 25-26
    student learning statistics, 20
    teacher beliefs, 22-24
    teacher engagement, 28-32
    teacher evaluation reform, 21-22
    teacher evaluation statistics, 20
    teacher evaluation system, 30-33

Teacher Evaluation System
Design, 33*f*
teacher trust, 32-33

Daily Tracker, 16-17*t*
Danielson, C., 8, 43-44, 72, 83, 84, 96,
114, 119-120
Data collection:
instructional leadership skills, 52-54
professional conversations, 92-93
professional self-assessment, 69, 70*f*
Davenport, T., 26
District office role:
action tools, 120-121
classroom visit, 113
educational reform impact, 107, 116
Framework for Teaching, 119-120
importance of, 105-106
Inquiry Team model, 116
Instructional Leadership Inventory,
120-121
key points, 120
leadership accountability, 106-107
leadership teams, 110-111, 112,
116-118
New Leaders Institute, 119
New Professionals Institute, 119
principal autonomy, 109-110
professional development,
112, 115-120
reflection questions, 122
school-goals alignment, 112-113
superintendent case study, 107-120
teacher evaluation system, 113-115
teacher experience, 107-109
vignette, 106
Dweck, C., 11

Educational Leadership, 37
Enhancing Professional Practice
(Danielson), 43-46, 72, 84, 96, 114,
119-120
Esterfield Unified School District,
109-120
Evans, R., 35

Feedback. *See* Constructive feedback
Fixed mindset:
leadership traits, 11-12
professional conversations, 93
Fletcher, M., 88-89
Framework for Teaching, 43-46, 72, 84,
96, 114, 119-120
Fullan, M., 12

Growth mindset:
leadership traits, 11-13
professional conversations, 93
Guiding Questions for Conversation,
98*t*, 103

Habits of mind, 7, 15
Harvard Education Letter, 10, 55
Historygram process:
culture of learning development,
28-30
guidelines for, 37-38*f*
How the Brain Learns (Sousa), 57
Human Side of Change, The (Evans), 35

*If You Don't Feed the Teachers, They Eat
the Students!* (Connors), 71
IMPACT system (Washington, D.C.), 21
Inquiry Team model, 116
Inquisitive listening, 57
In Search of Evidence handout,
60-61, 63*f*
Instructional leadership:
action tools, 60-61, 63*f*
effective teaching criteria, 43-46
Framework for Teaching, 43-46, 72,
84, 96, 114, 119-120
In Search of Evidence handout,
60-61, 63*f*
key points, 59-60
knowledge of staff, 40-43
necessary dispositions, 9-11, 12-13
reflection questions, 60, 61*f*
reflective learning, 47-48
staff retention, 42-43
staff selection, 39-40
student engagement, 48-51
teacher evaluation system, 46-47
Teacher's End of Year Reflection, 62*f*
teaching standards, 43-46
vignette, 41, 44-46
Instructional Leadership Inventory,
120-121
Instructional leadership skills, 51-59
classroom observation, 52-54
coaching, 54-55
constructive feedback, 57-58
data collection, 52-54
listening skills, 56-57
professional conversations, 52, 54-55,
85-87
professional goals development,
58-59
questioning skills, 55-56

Instructional practice:
  action tools, 76-81
continuous improvement cycle, 68-71
effective practice components, 67
expectations, 65-66
Framework for Teaching, 72
key points, 75
leadership teams, 71-72
professional development, 68-75
professional goals, 69-71
Professional Learning Plan
    Development, 69, 76*f*
professional training model, 73-75
  reflection questions, 75
  Research Roundup, 76
  student engagement, 68, 76, 81*f*
  teaching standards, 67
  transparency, 66-71
Instructional Practice Self-Assessment
    Form, 77-80*f*
Instructional Rounds, 87
Islands of competence, 90, 99

Journal of Educational Administration,
    95-96
Journal of Staff Development, 37
Judgment, 56

Keeling, D., 31
Knight, J., 24
Know Can Do (Blanchard, Meyer, and
    Ruhe), 112
Knowledge of staff, 40-43
Knowledge workers, 26-27

Lake Wobegon effect, 21
Leadership:
  accountability of, 106-107
  culture of learning actions, 32-35
  culture of learning role, 22-28
  positional leadership, 85-86
  See also Instructional leadership;
      Professional conversations
Leadership meetings, 97
Leadership teams:
  district office role, 110-111, 112,
      116-118
  instructional practice, 71-72
Leadership traits:
  fixed mindset, 11-12
  growth mindset, 11-13
  habits of mind, 7, 15
  instructional leadership role, 9-11,
      12-13

  managerial role, 8
  moral courage, 6-7, 13-14
  role clarification, 8-10
  self-confidence, 10-11
  self-perception, 7-10
Learning 24/7, 20
Listening skills:
  autobiographical listening, 56-57
  criticism, 56
  inquisitive listening, 57
  judgment, 56
  solution listening, 57
  unproductive patterns, 56-57
Listening Skills Inventory, 102-103

Managerial role, 8
Marlowe, Bruce, 69-70
Meyer, P., 112
Mindset (Dweck), 11
Moral courage:
  examples of, 13-14
  leadership traits, 6-7, 13-14
Moral Imperative of School Leadership, The
    (Fullan), 12
Mulhern, J., 31

New Leaders Institute, 119
New Professionals Institute, 119
New Teacher Project, 31
No Child Left Behind Act (2001), 107

Obama, Barack, 107
O'Neill, J., 28

Page, M., 69-70
Passaic Valley School District, 6-7
Professional conversations:
  action tools, 102-104
  classroom visit, 87-88, 95-97, 98*t*,
      99-101, 103
  Classroom Visit Log, 104*f*
  constructive feedback, 96, 99
  data collection impact, 92-93
  facilitation skills, 94
  growth mindset, 93
  guiding questions, 96, 98*t*, 103
  impacting factors, 89-94
  instructional leadership role,
      52, 54-55, 85-87
  instructional leadership skills,
      52, 54-55
  islands of competence, 90, 99
  key points, 101-102
  leadership meetings, 97

Listening Skills Inventory, 102-103
  opportunities for, 95-96
  positional leadership role, 85-86
  postobservation conference, 89, 97,
     99, 100-101
  powerful conversations, 83-85
  prerequisite conditions, 85-89
  process guidelines, 99-101
  professional development level, 91
  protocol for, 97, 99-101
  purpose clarification, 87-89
  reflection questions, 102
  school culture impact, 91-92
  teacher experience, 84-85, 88-89
  teacher rapport, 90
  teaching toolbox, 91
  topics for, 96-97, 98*t*, 103
Professional development:
  district office role, 112, 115-120
  growth model, 69, 70*f*
  instructional practice, 68-75
  leadership teams for, 71-72
  ongoing support, 118-120
  professional conversations, 91
  Professional Learning Plan
     Development, 69, 76*f*
  self-assessment data, 69, 70*f*
  time management, 118
  training model, 73-75
Professional development goals:
  goal-setting form, 78-79, 80
  instructional leadership skills, 58-59
  instructional practice, 69-71, 78-80
Professional journals, 37, 49, 95-96
Professional Learning Plan
    Development, 69, 76*f*
Psychology in Schools, 49

Questioning skills, 55-56

Race to the Top initiative, 3-4, 21-22,
    107, 116
Reflective learning, 47-48
Reilly, M., 86
Research Roundup, 76
Results Now (Schmoker), 19
Romano, M., 107-109
Rose-colored-glasses phenomenon:
  action tools, 16-17
  characteristics of, 1-7
  Daily Tracker, 16-17*t*
  educational reform, 3-4
  effective leadership traits, 6-14

habits of mind, 7, 15
key points, 14-15
moral courage demonstration, 6-7
parental perspective, 2
principal perspective, 3
red flag warnings, 3-6
reflection questions, 15
Teacher Evaluation Survey, 16, 17*f*
teacher evaluation system, 3-7
teacher perspective, 2-3
vignette, 1-2
Ruhe, D., 112

Schlechty, P., 111
Schmoker, M., 19
School culture, 91-92
Self-assessment:
  instructional practice, 77-80*f*
  professional development data,
    69, 70*f*
Self-confidence, 10-11
Self-perception, 7-10
Sergiovanni, T., 32
Sexton, S., 31
Shaking up the Schoolhouse
  (Schlechty), 111
Shulman, L., 47
So Long, Lake Wobegon? (Center for
  American Progress), 20
Solution listening, 57
Sousa, D., 57-58
Spaced-repetition technique, 25-26
Stanford University, 9
Student engagement:
  car metaphor, 48, 50-51
  cognitive engagement, 49-51
  defined, 49
  instructional leadership, 48-51
  instructional practice, 68, 76, 81*f*
  intellectual involvement, 50
  mental engagement, 50

Talk About Teaching (Danielson), 8, 96
Teacher Evaluation 2.0 (New Teacher
  Project), 31
Teacher Evaluation Survey, 16, 17*f*
Teacher evaluation system:
  culture of learning development,
    30-33
  district office role, 113-115
  educational reform, 21-22
  instructional leadership, 46-47
  Lake Wobegon effect, 21

moral courage impact, 6-7
performance standards, 46-47, 67
research statistics, 20
rose-colored-glasses phenomenon,
    3-6
Teacher Evaluation System Design, 33*f*
Teacher retention, 42-43
Teacher selection, 39-40
Teacher's End of Year Reflection, 62*f*
Teacher trust:
    culture of learning development,
        32-33
    professional conversations, 90
Teaching toolbox, 91
Thinking for a Living (Davenport), 26
Three Minute Classroom
    Walkthrough, 87
Topics for Conversation, 98*t*, 103

Transparency, instructional practice,
    66-71

Understanding Student Engagement, 81*f*

"Virtues of School Leadership, The"
    (Sergiovanni), 32

Webster Central Schools, New York,
    31, 34*f*
Weisberg, D., 31
"What Can We Do About Teacher
    Resistance?" (Knight), 24
"Why Great Teachers Stay" (Williams), 42
Widget Effect, The (Weisberg, Sexton,
    Mulhern, and Keeling), 31
Williams, J., 42
Wisdom of Practice, The (Shulman), 47

CORWIN

A SAGE Company

The Corwin logo—a raven striding across an open book—represents the union of courage and learning. Corwin is committed to improving education for all learners by publishing books and other professional development resources for those serving the field of PreK–12 education. By providing practical, hands-on materials, Corwin continues to carry out the promise of its motto: **"Helping Educators Do Their Work Better."**